A GRACE GIVEN

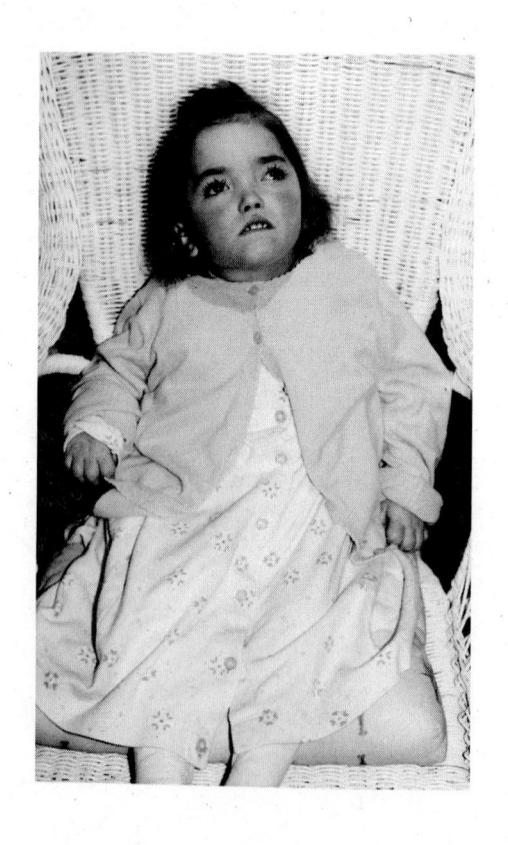

Elizabeth Nyanga Gilges

A GRACE GIVEN
Kent Gilges

CIDER PRESS PUBLISHING

A Cider Press Book

Published by
Cider Press Publishing
P.O. Box 262
Canandaigua, NY 14424

Copyright © 2008 by Kent Gilges

Second Printing

All rights reserved. No part of this book may be reproduced or transmitted in any form or by any means, electronic or mechanical, including photocopying, recording, or by any information storage and retrieval system, without the written permission of the Publisher, except where permitted by law: Cider Press Publishing, Canandaigua, New York.

ISBN: 978-0-615-17626-0
Library of Congress Control Number: 2007908831

Book design by Robert Kiesow
Interior layout and type design by G.L. Kriesen

Manufactured in the United States of America

www.ciderpresspublications.com

FSC
Mixed Sources
Product group from well-managed
forests and other controlled sources
Cert no. SW-COC-002512
www.fsc.org
© 1996 Forest Stewardship Council

The paper for this book was printed on 100% recycled, chlorine free paper produced with bio-gas energy.

For Liz

Acknowledgments

I am particularly indebted to my editor, Suzette Norris, who provided much of the final structure, the title, and other excellent suggestions for this book, to Bob Kiesow, whose design met my single requirement of 'simple' with beauty, to Reverend Robert Connor, whose generosity of spirit and enthusiasm pushed me to pursue publishing this book, and to my parents Pat and Walter Gilges, Liz's parents, Bette and Frank Russo, and our extended family, who made it possible for us to care for Elie the way she needed. I would further like to thank once again the many, many nurses, doctors, and other caregivers who made Elie's life as comfortable as possible. To my colleagues at The Nature Conservancy who helped me keep my family together, particularly Bill Weeks and John Sawhill, whose leadership was all about taking care of their people, and to Bill Ginn who supported the sabbatical to Brazil that allowed me to finish this book, many thanks. To Wendy Wagoner, who nursed Liz and me over a year, you have our eternal gratitude. Lastly, I would like to thank my children, Elie, Alexander, Nicholas, Oliver, Hannah and Avery, who make life truly wonderful, and my wife, Liz, who is one of the best things that ever happened to me.

Foreword

The author describes *A Grace Given* in his introduction as a "book about hope." It is surely that, but the description is almost too trite, too facile. The story here lets us for a short period see through the thin veil that separates the ordinary world from the divine. In that way, this is a startlingly religious book and is, itself, something of a grace given.

To read it is to experience the truth of St. Exupery's renowned secret dictum: *"It is only with the heart that one can see rightly; what is essential is invisible to the eye."* [1]

It is a documentary, or perhaps a diary, written by a self-avowed, "non-religious" person over the course of 13 years that gives testimony to how a kind and loving God intercedes in the daily lives of ordinary people.

What is most striking here is to find oneself caught up in emotion such that makes reading passages from the book in public all but impossible. I have used several passages in preaching retreats to various assemblages of both men and women, and I invariably find myself

---

[1] Antoine de Saint-Exupery, "The Little Prince" Harcourt Brace Jovanovich (1943) XXI, 70-71.

unable to continue because of the emotional charge that builds within me.

Before Kent wrote the book, I became privy to a short blurb he had written for a family newsletter that caught my eye. He said there:

> *At times, I have sensed in other people the belief that it would be better for Liz and me if Elie were to die soon. They feel she is a hardship, that it would make our lives easier, or more steady if she were gone, that it would strengthen our marriage by giving us more time together, less stress.*
>
> *I think these people are fools. I was right when I was a boy. Suffering is a gift.... Elie is the greatest gift we have ever been given. She makes our lives far richer, more contemplative, and full of joy than they ever would have been without her. She is a beloved—even essential—addition to our home and will be as long as she is with us. Elie has given us an awareness of suffering's noble beauty.*

Later, I read the eulogy he had prepared in anticipation of Elie's death. The interior emotion of the father invaded me as he recounted the fact that he prepared a eulogy for his child on an ongoing basis over 10 years. Imagine the sorrow of living daily with the impending death of the first child.

He goes on to mention—for me—the profound point that this child was held for her entire lifetime. She was affirmed tactilely by a certain number of persons, and he names them and says, "We touched her physically. She touches us spiritually."

God asks us as Christians to value two things above all else. First, love the Lord God with all your heart and soul. Second, love thy neighbor as thyself. This is a book that intimately describes love and the alchemy of sorrow. It reaches deep into the midst of pain and suffering and pulls from them the beautiful blossom of love and the gift of self. Where could we expect to find a love more intimate or generous than the love of father for child? But to expose that love so nakedly and unreservedly is a true gift.

It is difficult not to dig deeply into what is going on in the book and in the reader. We are dealing with a knowing that is in the heart and the emotions. In an apparent contradiction to scientific objectivity that reduces and analyzes reality into bundles of empirically measurable facts—a procedure to which even modern physics has given the lie—Kent Gilges has crossed the forbidden threshold of a totally disabled child and done the scientifically impossible: he "understood" her. By that I mean that he *"read her from within."* The etymology of the Latin *intellegere* is precisely *ab intus legere*.

Kent Gilges is a child himself peering into the persona of his beautiful daughter, and resonating with her, tells us who she is by telling us who he is. One becomes the father only by "becoming"—that is, residing in and knowing—the child. It would be fitting to dedicate this book to the reader who is a "Leon Werth *when he was a little boy"* in the manner that Saint-Exupery dedicated "The Little Prince."

For me, one of the most stunning parts of the book is the chapter "A Day in the Life" that describes the view of the world by the child as she could never in life have described it. It is the father putting himself into his child for a moment as she lies in the bathtub, held gently by his own hand. The father speaks to us through the child, gives voice to her, and connects her back to God.

But, who is this father who is inside this little girl's head and heart? Louis Evely suggests that only one who has suffered knows how to see. When you are young you are hard, selfish and protected. You have ups and downs and moods that have mainly to do with the affirmation that you are receiving. Ultimately, in youth it is all about you, and the compassion you might feel for others is gratuitous, generous perhaps, but superfluous.

But when you become a father, you suddenly become vulnerable in the most sensitive part of your being. "To become a father is to experience an infinite dependency on an infinitely small, frail being, dependent on us and therefore omnipotent over our heart."[2]

To be needed is to be loved. We all have that desperate need in order to achieve our own identity. Made in the image and likeness of the Son of God who reveals Himself to be sheer dependence on the Father, we most literally cannot be ourselves unless we are engendered by love. As Josef Pieper wrote: "It does not suffice us simply to exist; we can do that 'anyhow.' What matters to us, beyond mere existence, is the explicit confirmation: It is good that you exist; how wonderful that you are! In other words, what we need over and above sheer existence is to be loved by another person."[3]

As we read this story, it is true for the child. But it is even more true for the father. Again, Louis Evely:

> To love a person is inevitably to depend on him, to give him power over us. God loved us freely; God gave us power over him. God wanted to have need of us. The passion is the revelation of our terrible power over God. He surrendered himself to us, we had him at our disposal, we did with him what we wanted. On a plaque in Normandy one can read this cruel sentence: 'It is always the one who loves the least who is the strongest.'
>
> It is always he who is least in love who gets his way with the other, who keeps a cool head and stays in control of the situation. God, in regard to us, will always be the weakest, for he loves. God can be denied, forgotten; he cannot deny us, forget us. We can be without God. God cannot be without men.[4] We can stop being sons; he

---

[2] Louis Evely, "Suffering" Herder and Herder (1967) 127.
[3] Josef Pieper, "Faith, Hope and Charity," Ignatius (1997) 174.
[4] This refers to God's Erotic Love that is one with His Agape. See Benedict XVI's "Deus Caritas Est," #9-11. God's Love not only gives Self but desires (spousally) to receive free love from created human persons.

> *cannot stop being a Father… Thus, God will always be the weakest against us for he loves us.*[5]

Prior to his election as pope, and while taking part in the Second Vatican Council, Cardinal Karol Wojtyla wrote his last dramatic work, *Reflections on Fatherhood*. It provides a good summary for this work:

> *"And in the end You could put aside our world. You may let it crumble around us and, above all else, in us. And then it will transpire that YOU remain whole only in the SON, and He in You—whole with Him in YOUR LOVE, Father and Bridegroom*
>
> *"And everything else will then turn out to be unimportant and inessential, except for this: father, child, and love.*
>
> *"And then, looking at the simplest things, all of us will say: could we not have learned this long ago? Has this not always been embedded at the bottom of everything that is?"* [6]

Father, child, and love. That is what this book is about. Yes, it is about hope, but it is about much more than that to me. It is about what is most essential, and it is about allowing the eye to see what is most often invisible.

Reverend Robert A. Connor
Upper West Side, New York

---

[5] Louis Evely, "Suffering" op. cit.
[6] Karol Wojtyla, "Reflections on Fatherhood," University of California Press (1987) 368.

Contents

INTRODUCTION	1

❦ PART I

CHAPTER 1 Names	7
CHAPTER 2 Prophecies	15
CHAPTER 3 Oxford	29
CHAPTER 4 Spring Crocuses	39
CHAPTER 5 A Picture	49
CHAPTER 6 Reconciliation	57
CHAPTER 7 A Day in the Life	71
CHAPTER 8 Hope Rekindled	77
CHAPTER 9 Nine West	91
MIDDLE INTERLUDE	107

❦ PART II

CHAPTER 10 Waiting	121
CHAPTER 11 Recovery	129
CHAPTER 12 Time Flies	139
CHAPTER 13 Purgatory	145
CHAPTER 14 Lourdes	155
CHAPTER 15 The Velveteen Child	175
CHAPTER 16 Faith, Hope, and Charity	185
CHAPTER 17 False Expectations	193
CHAPTER 18 Private Thoughts	205
CHAPTER 19 John Paul	209
CHAPTER 20 John Paul II	231
CHAPTER 21 Requiem	243
CHAPTER 22 Miracles	247
CHAPTER 23 Purposes	257

Introduction

This is a book about hope. And love. It is about sorrow, anguish, joy. It is about a dying child named Elie. Most of all, though, it is about hope.

The course of our lives lies along a path that we travel alone. And yet our path crosses many other paths, more than we can ever reckon. Some join us for a time, others cross briefly. But in human terms, we travel the whole course alone, and how we interact with those many other lives around us, how we touch the world at large, is at least as important a measure of our humanity as how we carry ourselves in our solitary struggles.

I wish I could put the lessons that Elie has taught me at the beginning. I want the reader to know early what I have learned from her, from her tiny, insignificant, monumental life. I want these conclusions first so that I can draw the reader into the learning process itself. How she has taught me is at least as important as what she has taught me. Yet the lessons are in the learning. I do not believe anymore that wisdom is a point we reach but an understanding of the process we follow.

As I write this introduction, I sit on a Saturday afternoon beside my wife in our pediatrician's waiting room. Liz holds twenty-eight pound Elie on her lap, a child with a scarlet flush brushed on the silken cream of her cheeks, strawberry blond hair, lovely green eyes, red socks. Her feet are crossed and dangle against my wife's leg. Her hands twist awkwardly inward, a result of the tone that affects her musculature. Were she able to clap she would smack the backs of her hands together. But she will never be able to clap; a brain tumor and a stroke make that impossible.

Elie is peaceful and beautiful when she sleeps and often catches the eye of passers-by, but her disabilities are apparent to one who looks closely. Her eyes move independently of each other. Her head tilts back at an unusual angle. Beneath her dress, she has a tube in her stomach. Many people ask questions when they notice these differences. Some are afraid to. It is awkward for people to discuss serious illness in a child, much less to broach the idea of a limited future. Children are our symbol of hope in life. Hopelessness in a child is a painful anomaly. Hopeless hope. It is something we do not want to think about because it forces us to question ourselves, our lives, even God.

Today Elie has a 102.4 degree fever and we are fighting the most recent of a series of infections that strings back behind us nearly two years to the day a neurosurgeon in a hospital in the lower east side of Manhattan removed part of a tumor in the center of her brain. That she is still alive at all is due to him. And to Liz, who has kept her alive on love as only a mother could.

This story is about more than Elie. Yes, it is about others too. Part of the learning is that the story enfolds all those whom Elie has touched. It is about a Roman princess and the Pope. It is about the woman in a wheelchair, splashed through the window of a boat. It is about the prayer chain in Minnesota. It is about a four-pound girl's open-heart surgery and her mother's fight to keep her in a good hospital. It is about the Catholic priests that surround and pray for Elie. It is about me and my father, and Liz. It is about Elie's family. All of them, wide and near. That is why it is about hope. Because they are all her family. She has drawn them together; tied spiritual knots between their disparate lives.

There is a difference between death and dying. Montaigne said, "It is not death, it is dying that alarms me." Death is a result, dying is a process. We spend our lives dying, but the process of dying is what gives life its poignancy, its beauty, even its joy.

In one sense, death is easy to deal with. It happens. It is over. We, the living, are forced by life to let death go and we accomplish that through grief. But it isn't until we have grappled with dying, the long, slow dying of a loved one, that we are able to really see the remarkable beauty of life.

And a child dying. One's own precious, breathing child. I could never hope to describe that, nor impart a modicum of the desolation that bears down upon those of us who experience it. Perhaps I should not try. The future dies with the child, and yet the dying is a passport to life. The indomitable spirit rises up. Life bursts out of the dying process. Even with one's own child, life comes bubbling, searchingly to the surface. And life is different, raw, stripped, pure, clean. It is elemental. One comes up from drowning, baptized in the beauty of life.

Richter said, "The darkness of death is like the evening twilight; it makes all objects appear more lovely to the dying." Until we face loss, until we feel loss, we cannot fully understand beauty. Beauty is the handmaiden of loss, and the joy that transcends loss.

Pearl Buck wrote of her severely disabled daughter, "There must be acceptance and the knowledge that sorrow fully accepted brings its own gifts. For there is an alchemy in sorrow. It can be transmuted into wisdom, which, if it does not bring joy, can yet bring happiness." Just so. And yet the joy is there. Irrational as it sounds, time and our willingness to see sorrow as a hidden blessing are the key to the alchemy of joy. There is a blessing sent from God in every burden of sorrow. There is hope in that, hope even in a dying child.

This is the story of Elie and of joy and most of all of hope.

Part I

CHAPTER 1
Names

It is a long, cold walk on a frozen bay in mid-February. The wind lashes the ice, drifts snow up in low welts, carries it into the air around us. It is overcast and the sun is a hazy, heatless glow, low in the sky, the air so cold it freezes moisture in the eyelashes. Where the wind has stripped the surface, the ice is black and perfectly transparent. Looking down from directly above, we see ripples in the sandy bottom, a sunken log, then the bottom drops away into darkness and we are left with an eerie, vertiginous feeling.

In the center of the bay, there is nothing but the wind and an infrequent ping—like the sound of a metal stick hitting a high-tension wire—as pressure cracks form in the expanding ice. The sun in the west is no longer warm at all, and the wind rides down its tails, numbing our faces, tightening our jaws if we turn towards it. It is eight months since the day Liz called me, frantic, because Elie had gone limp on her right side. Eight months and a lifetime away, and this walk, this journey to the middle of the bay has become my metaphor for existence.

I walk in the cold to the center of the bay, half wanting to shout, half wanting to stand desolate in the middle of desolation itself. I want to stand in the middle of the bay where there is nothing between me and God. The sun, my metaphor for God, is up there, but hidden and distant. It gives no warmth. As I walk, the blackness yawns beneath the ice, yet I am held above it by something I cannot see, much less trust. When I finally reach the center and can howl my anguish in the wind, I am already spent, my will is gone, my face and body half-frozen by cold and the overwhelming sense of loss. I stare at the sky, feel the wind, shrug tiredly at my father beside me and turn back toward home.

These are the solitary moments that test our love and our loved ones. For me, there is nothing to do but carry on, love the child that God has given me, long to kiss her cheek even in the few moments when we are separated. For my father, there is nothing to do but walk with me, ask no questions, turn and walk back. This is my course, my life path, my sorrow. It is something I cannot share. Yet we share the moment. He has his own sorrow. As a grandfather watching his first and only grandchild dying, he has his own grief, and I cannot share that. We can only share the moments together, the actual fact of our separate existences crossing. His sorrow and my sorrow, occurring simultaneously, yet never the same, never something we can really share.

Liz and I are just so. We take turns being swallowed by desolation, like riding in the prow and stern of a pitching sailboat. As I plunge into despair, she rides up to the crest of a wave, stretches out a hand, touches my cheek until the roles are reversed. It goes on and on. I can be laughing one moment only to realize with a jolt what life will be like when I can no longer breath the ineffable fragrance of my daughter's hair, no longer nestle my nose into her neck; all joy in life drains away like spilled blood in sand and I plunge into the trough.

It is a hard course.

Elizabeth Nyanga Gilges was born on September 3, 1993. Full of surprises from the first, she emerged into the world a month early and a thousand miles from home. We had moved to a rural town on the edge of civilization in Michigan's great, forested Upper Peninsula. It was our sole purpose to raise a family away from cities. To my great chagrin, Elie jumped ship early and was born in the heart of urban New Jersey, two hours prior to the wedding ceremony we had traveled to New York to attend.

Even at this early stage, I see the two forms of God at work. On the one hand, He is the "Cosmic Humorist," the "Great Practical Joker," confounding our expectations, toying playfully with the ideas and principles we hold dear, forcing us to realize that in a pinch, most of it is unimportant. On the other hand, He is the "Great Plan." Somehow, and in some way I probably still do not understand fully, it was important that Elie was born in New Jersey. Her first week of life—for a week was all we could stay before returning to Michigan—was spent in the arms of each and every member of both of our immediate families. She was never put down. Indeed, she has seldom ever been put down since. But that first week, in Liz's family home with my family all visiting and staying just around the corner with friends, that first week was a chance for everyone to meet the child that would change all of our lives.

And it was important in another way, for her birth caught us so by surprise that we had not chosen a name for her. We may have expected a boy, I can hardly remember now, because we had two boys' names already picked out. Alexander and Oliver. But we had no name for a girl. I remember sitting beside Liz in the hospital room after they had taken the newborn with her mottled skin to be cleaned and swaddled. I asked her what we would name our first daughter. Liz rattled off a half-dozen names. I pondered.

"What about Elizabeth, after you?" I suggested.

She hesitated. "We have Elizabeths on both sides," she said, elated with the birth and her first child, not really able to concentrate yet on something as mundane as names. In fact, I pointed out, three of four grandmothers were named Elizabeth or a form of it. Mine were Liesel, who lived and died in Southern Africa, and Betty, the quiet, frail, strong-willed woman from Virginia. Liz's mother was Bette, and her mother's mother was Elizabeth. Once we had considered it, it seemed an inevitable choice.

Which left us the middle name to choose.

"Hannah," Liz said.

"That's the second girl," I said. "Hannah Rose. What about Catherine?"

"No. Then she'll be Elizabeth Catherine the Second."

"Sounds regal."

"I want something different."

"What about something from Africa. My family comes from there. And you and I have always thought about trying to live there sometime. Her middle name could remind us not to lose sight of our dreams."

Liz considered it, smiling impishly. "What was the name of that place you went? The name of the carved figure you brought back for me from Zimbabwe?" she asked.

"Nyanga," I said, "That's just what I was thinking."

"I wonder what it means?" she laughed.

"It's a place name. In the highlands. It's Shona."

"Let's do it. Let's name her Nyanga. To remind us."

"Everybody will hate it," I said laughing.

"So what?" she said. "Let's do it anyway."

Elizabeth Nyanga Gilges.

Liz loved picking out names. We have three dog-eared books at home with names and translations circled and highlighted, so we knew when we named the baby Elizabeth that it meant "God's oath."

Nyanga was different. It was a place I had been once with my father's sister, a beautiful place that I visited just after Liz and I began dating. I wanted Liz to see it too, for us to travel or live in Africa at some point, perhaps with our kids. I had been studying Shona as a sideline in graduate school, hoping vaguely to be able to use it sometime. I still had the soft notebook that I had bought to accompany tapes in the Oxford language lab. It had a much abbreviated dictionary in the back, and when we finally returned home, I looked up Nyanga. Laughing, I found two words that were close. One meant "horn of an ox." The second was defined as "witch doctor." Neither was exactly Nyanga, and we decided not to tell our parents the meaning. Late one night, I wrote a letter to my aunt in Swaziland and asked her to check with her gardener, who was Shona.

I was right. Our parents and everyone else hated her middle name from the beginning. In the hospital room, my mom said acerbically, "It probably means 'Place of the Vipers.'" Liz's cousin's wife from New Jersey wearing a velvet dress with a jabot, whispered to Liz, "Don't worry. You can change it until it's recorded on a birth certificate." Liz, fiercely loyal to my love of the name, said she didn't want to change it. Everyone shook their head. The poor girl. Can you imagine what her schoolmates will say?

A month later we received a blue Aerogram in a neat script. It was from my aunt Yvonne in Swaziland.

"...Spoke with Harrison about Nyanga. I never knew it had a translation. You remember the place, of course. We had the little cottage up there in the hills, near the Troutbeck Inn. Most beautiful place in Zim. Leopards in the hills and the waterfalls. It's a magical place. Anyway, Harrison said the best translation of Nyanga was 'Faith Healer.'"

God's oath. Faith healer.

I love my daughter's names. I don't really know why, but I do. They were the right names, given to us in a moment of inspiration.

Elie cried a lot right from the beginning. At first it was colic, or so we said. After about three months, we put it down to teething, though I note now, sardonically, that her first teeth came in at around 14 months. She could never be put down. She was bouncy, energetic. She hated to sleep. If we tried to put her down when she was crying, her cries would grow more and more frantic until, after only a few moments, we would enter her room to find her screaming with eyes wide in terror or pain. It was striking and unnatural, that terror, but she was our first and we knew no better.

We'll never know what caused those fits. Perhaps she was scared from her intermittent blindness. We realized later that her eyesight was probably better at times than others. Sometimes she could see us, though probably her vision was blurry. Other times, we don't think she saw at all. Perhaps when she cried or lay on her back, the pressure caused by the tumor on her optic nerve increased and her world went dark. A frightened six month old child screaming because she is left alone as her eyesight fades.

Or perhaps it was pain.

It is easy to ask if we should have recognized warning signs sooner. Our pediatrician said he spent three nights going through Elie's records to see if there was something he missed. It is natural to wonder, but not very fruitful. He had never seen a child with a tumor before. Nor had we. We did our best at the time, but cannot lay blame for our own inexperience.

And she could be so joyful. Lying in between Liz and me at 6 am with her hands in her mouth, wide awake and wide-eyed. She always had something in her mouth. We thought it was teething but maybe in the absence of sight, her mouth became her best sense. And as she lay there her hands grew cold and wet with spittle. "Guh," she said, almost like a grunt. "Guh." And then that sloppy, cold hand reached out and touched my back, waking me with a sudden start.

"Ah, Liz, why did you do that?" I yelped, whipping around in bed to find my wife beneath her covers, sleeping still, and a bright face, delighted with her position on the bed, kicking her feet and saying, "Guh."

I laughed out loud. "Oh, you little gem, Elie. Come here and let me warm those hands up." Cuddling around her small body, tucking her nearly hairless head into my chest, her legs and arms stretching out instinctively like a beetle on its back.

"Guh."

"Good morning, little girl."

          ❧ ☙

Her favorite game in the early months was horse. I sat her on my knee and bounced her to an old, German rhyme that my father loved to use with us. "Hoppe, hoppe, Reiter. Wenn er faellt, dann schreit er. Faellt er in den Graben, fressen ihn die Raben. Faellt er in den Zumpf, dann geht der Reiter, BUMPF!" And with that last word, I open my knees and let the baby drop down and bounce her bottom on the couch cushion.

Elie loved the horse game. We were very fortunate to receive a video camera from my parents that first Christmas, and Liz happened to capture the horse game on video one afternoon. Elie's face was framed against the bright light of our picture window. We sat with our faces about six inches apart. I held her hands and whispered urgently, "What's that, Elie? What is it? Do you hear it? What is it?" Her eyes stared at my nose and widened, and I began to bounce her on my knee. "It's a horse coming," I said, "It's a horse. Hear it. Hoppe, hoppe, Reiter..." And her smile was immediate and bountiful. She broke into a cackle and rode along with me, a little six-month old balanced precariously on my knee but held between my hands. "... Dann geht der Reiter, BUMPF!" And her eyes widened as she fell from the horse and was caught and lifted back up for a hug. Her laugh. Her delighted laugh is what I miss most.

And the translation seems almost prophetic now as I watch that tape, tears streaming down my face every time. "Hoppe, hoppe, Rider. When he falls, then he cries. If he falls in the grave, then the worms will eat him. If he falls in the swamp, then he goes down BUMP."

If she falls in the grave—and yet we catch her before she can fall. That is what we want as parents, all of us, to be able to catch our children before they fall. And yet their life path is their own. We can be there, but we may not catch them. Like my father walking on the bay with me. He could be there, but he couldn't catch me. It is my grief alone. Like Elie. I could hold her, but I couldn't keep the tumor out. It was her course alone.

CHAPTER 2
Prophecies

We have a religiously divided house. Liz was brought up a Catholic and has a very strong faith. Once, when I called a family conference (only she and I participated since Elie had already fallen asleep on the couch), I was struck by one of the answers she had to a question of mine. Our family conferences, at least the few that we have had, take the form of a series of paired questions such as, "What are the five nicest things that you do for me and vice-versa."

That night, one of the questions was, "What are the five most important things in our life." Usually it is uncanny how similar our answers are and how well we know each other. Highest on my list was Elie, followed by our health (particularly Liz and the new baby), our families, our health care plan, and some semblance of financial security.

The latter answers I was quite sure would differ, but I knew Elie would be first and our families a high contender. Wrong. Liz's list was, "1. God, 2. Our relationship, 3. Our Family, 4. Health, and 5. Friends." God was first on her list and didn't even make it into the top five on mine. I noticed that right away. Later that night when we were discussing it before falling asleep she said she noticed that I hadn't put her name on my list. My list was missing God and my wife. How strange.

I tell the story to illustrate the fact that I come from a non-religious family. It is not natural for me to speak about God, much less write about Him. I never attended church growing up, and in college I was an active disbeliever in organized religion. Yet one summer in Alaska I became certain of God's existence. An image floats in memory of a fishing boat skipper swilling beer, throwing the cans over the side, swearing at us in words I had never heard, sweeping a huge bear paw across the vista of bay, glacier, forested mountains, waterfalls, then pointing a finger at me and spitting out, "You honestly don't believe in God when you look at this." Me muttering something bookish but thinking if someone this putrid and low could be so certain of God, maybe I better take a closer look.

Belief growing from there. The waterfalls. The bear mid-river, catching salmon in their jaws. The mountains. God's mountains. And then the people. The goodness in people. And that little bit of faith took hold and grew through my college years into a firm and unwavering belief in God, the existence of God. The still unsettled question from there became "What form does God take." The All-Powerful. The Merciful. The Cosmic Humorist. The Great Plan. The Unknowable. The Man.

Asked as a question. Or all of the above?

Before Elie, the question of religion was one of the most difficult aspects of our marriage. I do not understand Catholicism, the many rituals and mysteries. To me, it seems contrived, ponderous. Teleologically, I find it difficult because of its adherence to the next world at the expense of this one. The mountains. The streams. Creation. Why would I want to focus on the next life when this one is so awesome?

I have since come to understand better the saying from Archbishop Fulton Sheen: "There are not over a hundred people in the U.S. that hate the Catholic Church. There are millions, however, who hate what they wrongly believe to be the Catholic Church." It is an easy religion to misunderstand and even easier to misrepresent.

Marriage, two people becoming one flesh, requires unity in the most fundamental things. For Liz, religion is one of the most fundamental, and it has always troubled her that it is an area about which we could not agree. I remain respectful, but I keep my distance. I attend church, but I have no desire to become Catholic. When she asks what religion I call myself, I consider my non-religious past, the fact that I sit in church every Sunday with a beautiful girl on my lap, and I respond that I must be a lapsed agnostic.

One of our neurosurgeons said that there are no atheists in the pediatric neurosurgery waiting room. Touched by that sudden need for support, we carry the belief in God beyond the crisis. Understanding that faith will ebb and flow over time, those who have been baptized by the fire of intense suffering and loss never totally forget that relationship built with God in the hours endured with a child lying on a hospital table, her tiny skull opened, out of reach.

And yet before any of this happens, we feel inklings of our religious needs. I am always surprised by the response of children to religion. When I was six or seven I remember wondering why my family didn't dress up and go to church like the other families around us. I also remember wanting to go and even asking my parents about it sometime near dawn one Sunday, "Dad, are we getting dressed to go to church today." I still remember the astonished face of my father as he sat up on the pillow and rubbed his eyes.

I am not alone. A friend's eight year-old boy, Anthony, approached his father one day as his dad and I sat on the porch. Out of the blue and to our mutual surprise, he said, "Dad, I think I want to become a priest." Then he wandered off again to play in the yard with his little brother and sister.

The reason these events surprise me is that the child's intuitive response to religion is so often positive. Up to a certain age, children in healthy families have not yet been programmed to be critical, to doubt, to disbelieve or mock. Their positive response, their will to believe seems to argue to me that the relationship to God which religion can represent is something that comes to us a priori. After hearing Anthony's comment, I drove home wondering if my own inability to be religious is a programmed response that blots out my better, natural impulse.

One winter evening in March 1994, I sat in a rocking chair, staring out the window of our living room. The night was black. There was no moon, but the sky was full of stars. I could just discern the lower limbs of the spruce tree outside the window. Liz was putting Elie, nearly seven months old, to bed, and I had been thinking all evening about religion and Catholicism. It struck me how important it was to Liz. Perhaps I should be more open to the possibility of religious feeling in spite of my lack of inclination. I decided to leave it up to God, so I sat in the chair and prayed: "God, if it is your will that I become a Catholic, if Christ has some relevance to me, and if religion is something that I should embrace, give me some kind of sign."

I stood and moved to the window, half-expecting a shooting star or some other dramatic event. I watched intently. The night was as black and quiet as any. Snow blew lazily over the drift just outside the window. There was no special sound, no unexpected movement. Nothing happened. Soon Liz called from the back and broke my reverie. She needed a clean diaper... could I help? I smiled at my moment's fancy and dropped back into my life as it was. How silly I was being, I thought. Soon, I forgot my request of God amidst the more mundane clutter of daily life, changing diapers, work, writing articles in the evening, fixing the house. It was easy to forget my prayer when nothing happened.

One month later, we found out Elie would die from a brain tumor.

∽ ↷

On April 20, Liz had an appointment with an eye specialist near our home. She had noticed that Elie had trouble seeing things at times and that one of her eyes tended to wander. We had read Doctor Spock, and were very concerned she might have a weak eye. Things seemed to get much worse when the doctor who examined her said he thought she might be cortically blind. He wanted us to see a specialist in Ann Arbor.

A few days later, Liz drove to Ann Arbor with Elie. I had business out of town but was scheduled to fly in to Ann Arbor the evening of the appointment, and then drive home the six hours with Liz and Elie.

I don't think I took the possibility of blindness very seriously. I had led a charmed life. A loving family. A good home. I had traveled all over the world. Lived in Italy and Germany. Liz and I had attended the best universities, had an idyllic honeymoon year in Oxford, gave birth to a beautiful girl. The world lay before me. Nothing really bad ever happened to me or my family. I must have assumed that the specialist would find something trivial. She wouldn't be blind. She only would need some extra therapy to strengthen the weak eye. It was a setback, though only a small one.

I arrived at the airport and looked around for Liz. She was not there yet, probably because she was having trouble finding a place to park. I wandered through to the pick-up area and waited. After 20 minutes I popped inside to call her college friend, Julie, who had put her up the night before. Julie answered. Her voice was subdued. She handed me off to Liz, who sounded shaken.

"Hi beautiful. Is anyone coming to get me?"

Liz started crying. "I tried to come, but I got lost, and the baby was crying, and I couldn't find it, and Julie wasn't at home so I was sitting outside in the car and I didn't know what to do."

"It's okay, Liz. Don't worry. Maybe Julie will come get me."

"I'm sorry, Kent."

"It's okay. How's the baby?"

"Kent." Long pause.

"Yes?"

"It didn't go well today."

"What do you mean? What's the matter? What didn't go well?" I realized suddenly. The appointment. I had forgotten all about it. I had known it would be okay, that we were being overly concerned new parents. The realization was quick and startling. "She's blind!" I said, "Oh, that's terrible. Does she have any sight at all?"

"We have to talk in person. I can't talk over the phone. Please hurry."

I hung up. I stared at the phone. It was not simple. It was not turning out okay. Something was wrong and I had another 20 minutes to wait. I dialed her parents' number. I knew she would have spoken to them since I was away.

"Frank. It's Kent. Is Bette there?"

"Yes, Kent. I'm here." They were both on the phone. Their voices were quiet, very serious.

"What's wrong? I'm stuck at the airport waiting for Julie and Liz says it didn't go well. What happened?"

Bette spoke. She had been crying. Bette never cried. "The doctor said he could see a mass."

"What do you mean a mass?"

She spoke softly. "Elie may have a brain tumor, Kent."

I stared at the chrome plating on the phone box. I jiggled the money return. Tears swelled up in my eyes and I had nothing to say. In that moment, everything went blank. My mind. My hopes. It was all blank and I was staring at the dull reflection of colors in the polished chrome of the telephone box. I traced the outline that the colors made. Bette went on talking but I didn't hear anything. I mumbled in response but have no idea what was said. I thought of my little girl with her wet fingers, lying between us in the bed. I leaned against the telephone box. "A brain tumor?" I said to myself, and Bette and Frank were both talking, trying to reassure me about God's will, telling me how much Liz needed me now, trying to calm a presence on the other end of the telephone who said nothing, did not respond, seemed lost. I was aware that around me people were carrying on, untouched by this crisis. The airport kept moving, the P.A. announced an incoming flight, the baggage conveyers swung around. Life was going on around me. I straightened up. A brain tumor.

And yet beneath that shock, the optimism was still there. It may not be a tumor. We don't know. Perhaps this doctor was wrong. He is only an ophthalmologist, after all. I needed to see Liz. I needed to know exactly what the doctor had said. How much certainty? What exact words did he use? Could it be something else? I hung up the phone and walked outside to wait for the car. A brain tumor. A mass. Cortical blindness. A weak eye. I felt very tired as I stood in the cold wind, waiting for a car. I wanted to go to sleep.

❧ ☙

Julie was leaving Ann Arbor that evening. She offered to let us stay at her house, but it was too crowded and uncomfortable. There was a single bed for Liz, Elie and me. I called a friend, an older woman who had given us a cottage to live in for the summer when we first moved to the Upper Peninsula. Marilyn was a gracious woman with a grandmotherly face touched always by a bit of sadness at the corners of her eyes. She had lost her husband to cancer two years before we met her, and talked about it often with us. Two years later, it still weighed heavily on her, accentuated by the need to pursue alone what had always been done with someone else in their little paradise up north. Camping, sailing, beach breakfasts. That first summer she had taken us blueberry picking at her favorite spot and had outpicked us single-handedly. We made blueberry pies in her kitchen and ate them on her lovely sun porch. She seemed a natural person to turn to for help. She knew Elie. She would understand this shock and grief.

Liz held the baby while I called Marilyn. She held her in the car as we drove across town and I searched for street signs. I answered her questions, mumbled reassurance, probably using the same words Liz's parents had used with me. Liz was crying and I was trying to comfort her. It was my job to remain in control, to comfort my wife, to find us a place to sleep. We arrived and rang the doorbell. Marilyn let us in; she had been crying. She hugged us and showed us to a room upstairs. She wanted to leave us alone. She told me where the phone was if I needed to make any calls. I thanked her. Liz sat on the bed with the baby. I felt so tired.

Then Liz had to use the bathroom. Could I hold Elie for a moment while she went? I picked Elie up mechanically, too tired to even think, but when her cheek brushed mine, when she snuggled up against my neck, the sudden realization of her dying struck me like a slap and I started to cry, hardly able to get a breath, sobbing as I stood rocking her and whispering, "My baby, my baby, my baby." I stood in the light of a bedside lamp, alone in the room with Elie and realized that my child, who cackled with delight when I nuzzled her collar bone, could die. It suddenly seemed possible and, though I would regain my optimism over the next few days, in that moment I knew what could happen, and I feared it.

※ ※

The following week is a blur. It is a medical phenomenon that following a sudden trauma, such as a fall or car crash, one often does not remember the event or the moments leading up to it. Almost as a protective defense, the mind forgets the trauma. Liz had scheduled an MRI, a magnetic resonance image, for the following week. The eye specialist wanted us to see a brain specialist. Elie was probably blind; she could also have a tumor.

We drove home to the Upper Peninsula. It was six hours, but I remember nothing of the drive. Liz kept saying that she could not wait a week to find out if her only child has a brain tumor. I didn't know why she had made an appointment so far in the future. She had been in shock. I knew what that was like now. I kicked myself for not having gone with her. I had to keep track of details. In the morning I woke with the same feeling as her. We couldn't wait a week to find out something as critical as this. I asked her for the appointment card. I would call and change it. Taking care of the details was my job.

The card gave an appointment two weeks away. I read it again and double-checked on the calendar. "This isn't next Wednesday," I told Liz. "It's two weeks."

I called the office number. The nurse who answered sounded harried but was sympathetic. "I'm sorry, though, Mr. Gilges. Two weeks from yesterday is the earliest available appointment. The MRI is under heavy demand and unless it is an emergency..."

"Don't you think that a brain tumor is an emergency?" I asked, hardly believing I had used the words to describe my daughter.

"I understand that is a long time to wait. I wish there was something I could do."

"Give us an earlier appointment. That's the one thing you could do. After telling us this, you can't expect us to wait two weeks."

"It must be difficult. I wish I could help you but that is really the earliest appointment."

I thanked her and hung up. I told Liz we would have to wait. I found my keys and left for work. I had better at least clear up loose ends at the office, though once there I could not think about work at all. Why were they willing to let us wait two weeks? Perhaps they thought the likelihood of a tumor was low, and that was why it was not urgent for them.

During that time and right up until the moment we received a definitive diagnosis, I nurtured hope in any event. They wanted us to wait two weeks. That must be good. Malignant. Benign. The two words that were largely undefined in my vocabulary at this point rose up. It must be benign or they wouldn't wait. Would I feel differently if they had rushed us in the following day? That would have meant malignant. On and on my reasoning went, as much to keep my mind occupied as to really understand. Building hope allowed me to avoid the one possibility that gnawed at me: my daughter could die.

It was only later, after months and years of dealing with medical personnel, hospitals, and doctors that I realized it is folly to attribute motives to them. They see children like Elie every day, day-in, day-out for their whole professional careers, little children with terminal illness. To the receptionist, I was just another worried parent on a long list of worried parents who wanted access to the MRI tomorrow. I know now that she and most of her counterparts would try to do what was best for me because she was sympathetic, but they have to continually manage those sympathies to be able to deal with so much pathos.

I say that they see Elies, children like her with crippling, mortal diseases, daily. And yet I must add that we have often remarked on the attachment that Elie alone has engendered among some of her doctors. They deal sympathetically with most parents and children, but some of the medical professionals—like many that have prayed for her, visited her, held her—have been extraordinarily attached to Elie. I try to pinpoint what it is that so draws people to her and to her alone, and even now I cannot. I think it has partly to do with her natural beauty, which is extraordinary. I think part has to do with how much we love her, openly and visibly, in thought and deed. I remember back to one night after Elie's surgery when she lay in a hospital crib with tubes and wires coming out of all parts of her. I left Liz sleeping on the fold out chair and stepped out at about 2 am to wander around the block and breathe some summer air. When I returned an hour later, I walked into the dimly lit room to see one of the oncologist residents standing beside the crib, watching my wife—who had crawled up into the hospital crib—sleep with her arms cradling Elie's legs. As he heard me enter, he nodded and left, and I noticed tears in his eyes.

At ten o'clock the following day my office phone rang. It was Liz calling from home. She did not wait for my normal greeting. She was crying.

"Kent. It's Elie. She can't move her right side. Her arm is limp. Kent, I'm so scared."

"Have you called the ambulance?"

"No. I don't know what to do. She's limp on one side. I don't want her to die."

Events around that time move in and out of focus. I have memories that are crystal clear—crying by Marilyn's bed, Liz lifting the baby's limp arm and letting it drop, the moment we were told the worst news of all—but the majority of memories are lumped together, out of focus. The time between days is not delineated. Two years later on another sudden visit to the emergency room, I recognized both the attending physician and the male nurse who helped us with the cat scan when we first rushed to the hospital that morning. I never would have remembered them if I hadn't seen them again, yet they were etched permanently in the hidden recesses of my mind. Perhaps all of the events around great trauma are like that. We remember them but hide them away. Then we uncover and deal with them when we can, when they are less painful. It is always easier to understand sorrow looking backwards.

The attending physician that day in emergency was worried about a stroke. He ordered a CAT scan. Elie was happy except that one arm and half her face did not work. She was busy sucking on her other hand. We waited a long time, and were finally told that they saw enlarged cysts in the middle of her brain. She had too much fluid, but they couldn't deal with that in northern Michigan. They would transfer us to Ann Arbor.

I asked about a brain tumor.

"Hard to tell," the radiologist answered. "These cysts could be related to a tumor. I would need a better scan. At least it doesn't appear to be a stroke or aneurism," he said guardedly. "Go to Ann Arbor where they have a pediatric neurosurgeon."

Hydrocephalus. Sub-arachnoid cysts. Tumor. Malignant. Benign. Meningitis. Masses. CAT scan. MRI. Contrasts. Gaudolinium. Aneurism. I felt desperately that I needed to understand all this as quickly as possible. I needed to know what they meant because I could be called on to make a decision on behalf of my daughter at any time. Should they operate? Is it urgent? What do all of these things really mean? Am I doing the right thing?

Over time, I have come to know and understand these things. Between Liz and me, we probably know brain diseases better than many doctor-residents. I take that back, we definitely know better than a resident. We may understand as much as a resident specialist. But you have to know. It is your child. You have to know to make a decision about her life because the decision and the results are what the parent must live with forever. The medical professionals will see this again in other children. It is not as urgent for them. They will forget this one. We will live with the decisions forever.

We were back in Ann Arbor three days after leaving Marilyn's. An ambulance had driven Elie to Ann Arbor. Liz held her on the gurney and I followed in our little Honda, watching them through the rear window of the ambulance. Shortly after checking into Mott Children's Hospital, my parents arrived. Liz's sister Kristin came. My brother flew in, followed closely by Liz's parents. They placed an I.V. They scheduled an MRI. Doctor after doctor came and took histories. We told the same story again and again. They told us about a patient's rights. They were very concerned for our welfare.

Elie lay in my arms with a gown on. She smiled crookedly and tried to put her fist in her mouth, but the board securing the I.V. line kept her arm straight. She sucked on the edge of the board. When we held her up, she stood on her wobbly legs. She laughed when I nuzzled her collar-bone. It didn't seem she could be sick, but her smile was lopsided. Half of her face was paralyzed. It was more than cortical blindness: we all knew that. But we hoped for the best.

An hour or two after the MRI we were all sitting around her. The mood was quite upbeat. Elie's eyes twinkled. She was chewing on her hand and saying, "Guh." People talked of other things, other places. We laughed. It was like sitting around the kitchen table in Liz's family home, everyone talking, being together, a family.

The resident specialist who came in looked troubled. He stood by the door for a moment.

Liz sensed him immediately. "What is it?" she asked. Our family seemed to step back from us.

I rose, "Do you have any results?"

He stepped into the room and shook hands with me. He was tall, well-built with short blond hair and glasses. He looked mid-western, clean-shaven. He said, "I'm the neurosurgeon resident. The attending pediatric neurosurgeon is looking at the scans now, but I thought you would be anxious for a preliminary report. She'll probably be an hour yet."

"What is it?" Liz said again. "It's bad, isn't it?"

"I'm afraid so," he said bluntly. "She does have a mass around the hypothalamus."

"She has a tumor?" I said.

"Yes. I don't know more than that. When the neurosurgeon comes, you'll get a better report. I thought you might want to know this much at least."

Jesus, I thought, I want to go back to cortical blindness. I want to go back to anything. I want to go back. This can't be happening. Elie has a tumor. Liz slumped into the chair and was crying.

"What kind of tumor?" I asked.

"It's massed around the hypothalamus," he repeated. "I don't know more than that at this point."

Our families stood by. Nobody said a thing. I looked up and saw my father crying.

"When the doctor comes, we'll have some more information," he added. "It should be less than an hour."

CHAPTER 3
Oxford

My mind drifts back and is filled with one of the happiest times in my life. It was 1990, we were just married and I was a student at Oxford. Many of the memories seem so distant now that they blend together and I am left with only snippets and the warmth of remembered joy. I feel as I reach back like I have awakened and remembered a dream, but the harder I focus on it the more it slips away. Only the feeling is left, the fullness of feeling and the memory of a high, rewarding beauty.

Our life together began with a jaunt to Italy, as I left a job in Boston and followed a vivacious, young student named Elizabeth Russo, who was studying art for a semester in Florence. I found a two-room apartment over the leather market in the city center and tried to write stories, but instead spent most of my time staring out the window, drinking wine, and romancing my future wife in the trattorias and side-street cafes of a romantic city.

In the evenings, I listened from my darkened window to the sounds of the market packing up, the heavy carts loaded and locked, then rolled past my window and through the massive wooden doors that fronted the buildings in the city. Life had a medieval feeling, as if the Medicis themselves might enter down

Via Rosina followed by their entourage on horseback, turn left at the market and file into the piazza before San Lorenzo.

As the evening light died, the strollers would emerge and pass beneath my window, wandering down past San Lorenzo and toward the restaurants behind the Duomo or the cafes near Piazza Nazionale. Liz and I would meet for supper in the restaurant across the street, and wander afterwards along the river with its many beautiful bridges, stopping for gelato or a movie.

When she left Italy, I moved north and did some freelance writing from Germany, France and the Netherlands. Wherever I went, I thought about Liz and the lovely afternoons we spent wandering through Fiesole, or the week in the Greek Islands, or the first few days when she met me in Milano and took me to the Italian coast, where we spent time in a small town called Cornelia. There we met to eat breakfast on an open-air porch that looked down on the Mediterranean and to take long walks along the coast. There, I knew I had fallen deeply in love.

In April I called her from a trip to Austria to let her know that I had been offered a permanent job in Germany. I could hear disappointment in her voice. It meant I would not come back to the United States as we had planned. I told her I was likely to be in Europe for a few years.

She said it sounded like a great opportunity. And almost in the same breath, she told me that she could not wait for me to come back to her. The combination of the palpable sadness in her voice and her willingness to let me pursue my ambitions without any sense of regret or recrimination touched me deeply. I realized I wanted never to make her unhappy and that I wanted her to share the adventure with me.

"If I take the job," I told her, "I think I would want you to come over here with me."

"You know I can't," she said.

"I know you can't now," I replied. "Who knows what the future may bring."

We talked about it a bit more and then I hung up, slightly dazed by what I had just suggested. I had not planned it at all, yet it was not something I wanted in the least to retract. I would marry Liz Russo at some point, of that I was certain.

And I did take the job, and I did return a few months later, and I did propose to Liz from the seat of a bicycle as we rode past the mill pond and toward the harbor in the Long Island town that had been her only home. I told her we probably would never have much money, that I wanted to see many places, wanted to live in Europe, Africa, the States. I told her that life with me would be a constant adventure, and that I wanted to share the adventure only with her.

And she accepted, saying that she would love to be my wife and to have many children with me. She told me then, as she had told me many times before, that it was her ambition to be a young mother and that she would follow me anywhere as long as our lives included children.

∾ ભ

Two years later, we lived in a graduate college on the banks of the languid Cherwell River amidst the splendor of Oxford University. I read during the day, attended lectures, played rugby in the Parks. Liz turned pottery, danced ballet, and bicycled to meet me in the late afternoons and attend my intercollege matches. It was almost too glorious to believe. I had been given a Rotary scholarship that was generous enough to cover living expenses for both of us. Liz worked a little to earn travel money that took us to Portugal, Wales, Devon and Cornwall, the Lake District. I won an essay contest that gave us enough money to travel to Italy for four weeks. I was earning a graduate degree. Life was uncomplicated and I was more challenged than I had ever been. It was a grand beginning to the adventure that I had hoped our lives would be.

I remember our friends and long hours in animated discussion. The conversations would turn over anything at all, from English football to politics to the merits of Irish beer. As the spirits flowed, someone would take a daring position and the argument would begin that could only end in uproarious laughter and friends bidding friends good night in the moist, midnight air. Then the walk across the lawns to our apartment.

We dined with others often. Never have I had such friends. Martin Nowak, the brilliant mathematician from Austria, who burst into the squash court one day and without a word whipped me three straight games. As we sat against the wall afterward, he said, "I was celebrating because I had another paper in Nature this month and I didn't even know it." The funny thing was at that point I didn't even know what he was studying. Our friends never talked about work or their studies. Only later did I read Martin's papers in Nature, which developed a mathematical theory about mutation in the AIDS virus. Martin was one of Europe's rising stars in science. Among friends, however, he was the squash and tennis fanatic.

Often we dined in hall. Unlike most Oxford colleges, ours, Wolfson, had an egalitarian social structure. There was no head table, no separate rooms for faculty. We shared a common room for sherry before and coffee after meals. The meals were not served, except on special occasions. Everything about living in college revolved around conversation. In fact, everything about Oxford, both academic and social, encouraged talk. If ideas and the ability to communicate them are the prerequisite of culture, Oxford breathed, shared, and infused culture.

Liz and I bicycled everywhere. To the Trout Inn near the ruined abbey, across Port Meadow, down the Broad Street, around the Sheldonian, and back up through North Oxford. We met for tea next to the covered market, carried our produce in baskets, rode north to Blenheim Palace with its woodland daffodils, and ate bread and double Gloucester along the river. In the evenings, we joined friends in their rooms or apartments for dinner, wine, and a good, heated argument, then the good-natured conversation that followed. I have never laughed as much as I did in Oxford.

I was like a sponge, soaking up the overflow of a percolating boil of intellectual energy. But more than intellect, I was captured by the stimulus of other people: Liz says it was Oxford that turned me from an introvert to an extrovert. How likely that is, I can only guess, but it was Oxford that made me enjoy listening to other people's ideas, learning about their strengths and their faults, enjoying my time with them. If I entered Oxford cynical—even a misanthrope—I left it a humanitarian. I left it in love with life.

Above all that, though, well above the level of self found or horizons broadened is the strength that developed through the power of a great, fulfilling joy remembered. In the worst of times, I hold as so much a part of my psyche that great wholeness that I felt once amidst a city of dreaming spires, that I can endure the great sorrows that come. Joy and the unity of my soul in that time provided strength for future grief and sorrow.

And as I consider that joy, I cannot help but wonder whence it came. The joy was not part of the city itself, which seems dour on first view, or even the colleges, which are merely intimidating to the uninitiated. The joy develops because of all that Oxford offers. It is an alchemy of intellectual curiosity, friendship, love, adventure, spiritual exploration, growth, and all of the many other blessings bestowed by that fair setting. As a university, Oxford is not about the pursuit of knowledge. It is about the pursuit of culture, of raising the human spirit to the heights meant by the Creator. To reach those heights, one brushes closer to that Creator than ever before in life, and the joy one feels is like the warm glow as we near a blazing hearth. That joy infuses through us. We do not create joy. Rather, we find it as we reach spiritually and intellectually for the potential that God has given us. Joy is the eternal, and reaching for the eternal brings us closer to God. In Oxford—and at times since—I brushed against the eternal, I felt joy. It is not an encounter from which one leaves unchanged.

Sheldon Vanauken, who writes movingly of his great happiness in Oxford and of the subsequent death of the wife who shared that time with him, describes a similar reliance on the memory of fulfillment in the past. The memory of joy becomes the strength which carries him through his grief over the death of his beloved wife, Davy.

In one of the most significant passages to me, a group of Vanauken's Christian friends are talking late in the night at their small apartment—just as they had done and loved to do so many nights before. Yet they were each beginning to think about plans beyond Oxford, for their terms of study were drawing to a close. Vanauken describes the scene:

> In a way, all of us knew, knew as an undercurrent in our minds, that it wouldn't last forever. Lew and Mary Ann expressed it one night by saying, 'This, you know, is a time of taking in—taking in friendship, conversation, gaiety, wisdom, knowledge, beauty, holiness—and later, well there'll be a time of giving out.' Later, when we were scattered about the world. Now we must store up the strength, the riches, all that Oxford had given us, to sustain us after.

∽ ∾

As we waited for the neurosurgeon, we bent over the bed, holding Elie. She was naked except for a diaper and the IV board on her left arm. She gnawed on her left fist, made delighted sounds, and smiled crookedly. I held Liz with one arm and helped her say the Rosary. It seemed like the only thing to do. I knew she needed it, needed something to cling to. I kept wondering if we could pray the tumor away. If we prayed desperately enough, would it change the outcome? I helped her say the Rosary, reciting the first part and letting Liz say the response.

Kent:

> *Hail Mary,*
> *Full of Grace.*
> *The Lord is with Thee.*
> *Blessed art Thou among women,*
> *and blessed is the fruit of Thy womb, Jesus.*

Then Liz:

Holy Mary,
Mother of God
Pray for us sinners,
Now and at the hour of our death, Amen.

The room was so still. Other than our words, only Elie made any noise. Behind us, I could hear the clicking of the beads in Liz's mother's hands as she followed along with us. In future I would hear the beads many more times, often accompanied by a sense of puzzlement as to their purpose, until, once, on a balustrade looking down on a candlelight procession of invalids at Lourdes, I heard them in Bette's hands behind me and suddenly they meant something to me as well. Now, however, I stood over my only child, repeating these phrases like an incantation and wondering if it could do anything at all for our child.

To this day, I do not know how Liz felt as we stood there in that interim between bad news and worse. Whether her belief in God's mercy gave her relief, whether she—like I—hoped that quick prayers, offered spontaneously, would somehow save us from the terrible tragedy that awaited, or whether she simply felt deserted and helpless. I do know that I had never felt so desolate. I was heading down a corridor toward tragedy and there was no way out. It was an inexorable walk towards tragedy. I knew it was coming, yet my heart couldn't accept it. I still wanted an alternative, and the only alternative was a miracle. So I clung to the remote possibility of a miracle. I clung to it that afternoon, I clung to it through the following weeks, then through numerous surgeries, then through a trip to Lourdes, and finally through many months of follow-up. I had no choice. It was either give up my only child, give up hope, or believe in the slightest possibility of a true miracle.

As if to echo my thoughts, Liz turned to me at one point and said, "We have to pray for a miracle now, Kent."

And we did. We both prayed for a miracle. That afternoon and every day hence we prayed that we would not lose Elie. Over time, many others, hundreds—perhaps even thousands—of people prayed with us. I don't know about the others, but I prayed for a specific miracle. I prayed for a cure. I thought if we were to get a miracle it would be sudden and complete. That my daughter would be healed and I would know God's existence. I waited for many months. In some ways, I am still waiting, though I no longer look for the miracle as I once did.

The real miracle, I have come to see, was something different than perhaps any of us had expected. It did not come suddenly, rather it grew into us. It grew into everyone who touched Elie. At the time, however, hunched over my daughter, I had no way of foreseeing this.

∽ ∾

The doctors, when they entered, entered as a group. We never heard them, so focused where we on Elie and the prayers. Bette touched my shoulder, and Liz and I turned around as the resident entered with the chief pediatric neurosurgeon and the chief pediatric oncologist. A social worker joined them.

Our room fell silent as they entered. The neurosurgeon was a short woman who walked with a limp and the heavy boot worn by someone born with a clubbed foot. She was plain, and blunt, and wore her hair short.

"It is not good news," she said as she put the MRI scans onto the light board.

We all fell quiet. Liz and I sat down. Bette took Elie from our arms.

The neurosurgeon stood by the scans. "You can see here," she pointed to one picture, "is a cross-section of your daughter's brain.

Each picture is like a slice moving from front to back. These scans here," she pointed to another set, "are taken vertically from top to bottom."

She paused to gauge our understanding. "The normal brain is the grey matter here. You can see it curves around behind. The black matter in the center is fluid. These are called the subarachnoid cysts. In a normal brain they would be much smaller and most of the space inside the head would be composed of brain. These cysts are quite large, and clearly the pressure they are creating on the brain has caused the brain to compact. It may be part of what has compromised her motor activity."

"Can you do anything about the fluid?" I asked.

She held up a finger. "The fluid is a minor issue," she said. "The major issue is this white mass at the center of the brain. Here." She pointed again.

We could see a white mass quite clearly.

"This is a brain tumor," she said quietly.

We waited. I no longer knew what Liz was doing, or anyone else in the room. It felt like the blood was rushing to my head and I could hear the blood itself pumping. I saw nothing. I shut my eyes and all that I was aware of was the voice of the doctor as she gave us the news. I could hear her clearly.

"It is a large tumor, about the size of a golfball, surrounding the hypothalamus in the center of the brain. It is probably malignant."

I realized that I didn't really know what all of this meant. All I kept thinking was, "It's bad. It's bad."

Liz asked, "Is it operable?"

"The hypothalamus is in the center of the brain. It is the area where the three main arteries that supply blood to the brain enter from the neck. It is also the area where the optic nerves meet. A resection is too dangerous. If we tried to remove the tumor, there is a high likelihood that we could kill her on the table."

I hadn't opened my eyes yet. I started to cry. Once I started I couldn't stop. My mouth opened. My body slumped forward. I wanted to ask how long but all that came out was a horrible, low whine. My face and lips were drawn back and frozen in place. It was the look of a man whose heart was breaking. I could not stop. I heard Liz's voice beside me. It was oddly calm and quiet. "How long will she live?" Liz asked.

I heard the doctor answer something about treatments, radiation, chemotherapy. I heard her talk about Elie's head getting larger and larger. She talked about pressure from fluids, the tumor, the rapid growth.

"How long," Liz asked again.

"Six days. Six weeks. Maybe six months. We're crystal-balling it at this point. Nobody knows for sure."

And then I felt Liz's arm over my back and her head against my shoulder. I heard her begin to cry, but could do nothing for her. I felt the warmth of her forehead against my neck, but I couldn't open my eyes, couldn't move my arms. I leaned toward her, but my chest was heaving and that horrible, wrenching whine emerged. Poor Elie, smiling, laughing, lovable Elie was going to die. I was going to lose my only child.

The doctors spoke for a while more but we heard none of it. They filed out. There was quiet again in the room. Our families retreated to a corner of the room and left us sitting next to each other in our chairs, holding each other, worn out. There was nothing to do. We could not avoid this. We could change nothing. We would lose Elie. We stayed in the chairs, leaning against each other until long-after the evening sun had set and the light had died in the sky, leaving our room and us in darkness.

CHAPTER 4
Spring Crocuses

The first crocuses bloom overnight at winter's end, drawing a distinct stage curtain between the seasons. Winter's sour grass and salt-dusted streets fold up neatly in a sleeper's rain, and the earth unbuttons a lawn full of flowers like careful gems.

Idleness is the Lord's Sunday blessing, and I spend my idleness photographing flowers in the late afternoon. Fragile crocuses, white and purple, yellow, lavender, here a veined and royal blue—they bloom over a long grass meadow within the park. The bare trees above have not yet caught the waft of spring air percolating through the soil. A girl writes nearby, letters buried in her crouched lap. Behind her, a single jet of water throws up a fountain in the duck pond. Across the water, two dozen old men and women line the row of benches wing-to-wing like herring gulls on a wharf.

I work quietly, a young man just out of college and living in Germany. The flowers themselves demand no intercourse. They wear silence under their vibrant colors like gliding swans. A man approaches as I steady my tripod and adjust the lens. He stands just at the edge of my attention. I look up and smile.

"Are you a good photographer?" he asks in German.

"No," I say in truth, "I'm not."

We chat together idly. He is a young man, and very gracious. The afternoon light lengthens. The air cools and a breeze drifts over the lip of the wall, numbing the park like a draught of spirits. I tell him about my home. He pulls a picture of his family from his wallet. It is almost too dark to see, but I make out a wife and a young girl with chocolate brown eyes and a bright smile. The wife, he tells me after a moment, died at Christmas. He studies my face intently, and I mumble that I am sorry.

A moment later, in the melancholy shadows, we say goodbye. He drifts away, having stopped only to knead his sorrow down against spring's bitter leaven.

I turn to the flowers again, but the light is well past gone. How quickly the spring light dies and the colors fade when one carries a burden in the heart.

∽ ↷

I wrote this when I lived in Germany—before Liz and I were married. It was one in a series of vignettes that I sent back to the public radio station in my hometown of Pittsford, New York. Before I left for Europe, the host for the morning show had asked me to read one of my essays. Once I was in Europe, I contacted him to ask if he would like more of the same. I faxed them to my father, who has a wonderful English accent and reading voice. My father agreed to visit the radio station once a week to read the essays on my behalf.

I only remembered this vignette after finishing the final paragraph of the last chapter of this book, and it took a while to find again. Yet with all the time that has passed, I can still remember the feeling of desolation and grief in the young German man who stopped to talk with me. Sorrow can be so crushing that we dare not keep it to ourselves. It is something that we, who are filled with sorrow, have to share. Much more than happiness, sorrow forces us to reach out to the first person who can listen and accept some portion of the sorrow. It feels at times that to have an overwhelming sorrow and no way to share it would burst our hearts.

At the time, I remember wondering why this young man so filled with sadness had chosen me to unburden himself of some small portion of his sorrow. Now I know. It is an intuitive choice. We cast around among friends, strangers, anyone to talk to until suddenly we realize we have found someone who could accept part of our sorrow. We know immediately those who could not, and this includes most people. But the few, or the one, who seem open to it, to them we unburden ourselves, let down our guards and tell our story.

I don't know how the young man knew I would take a part of his burden. I did not know myself. I think he just sensed it. Whatever aspects of the way I was working in the park, the lightness of my heart, my willingness to talk to a stranger, my mentioning my own home with a slight longing and homesickness that I'm sure he could sense, even the slant of the afternoon light and the coming twilight. All of these things let him know that this was the time and I was the person, and so he opened his heart to me, for a few brief moments, completely, unreservedly.

And I did take a part of his burden. I carried a part of his sorrow away with me that afternoon. On my bicycle ride home that night, I thought about his family, about him losing his beloved wife. I carried enough of his sorrow with me to write about it, and in this small way eased the sorrow for both him and me.

There is a phenomenon in quantum physics called Bell's Theorem. In simple terms it states that if two particles which are bound together could be taken apart and separated, even by great distance, and if you were to reverse the spin on one particle, the other would simultaneously change its own spin. The implication is that the two particles are part of a unified whole, and anything that affects the one affects the other.

In the relationship that developed between the German man and me, we became like the two paired particles. His contact formed the bond between us which allowed sorrow to shift, like a liquid seeking equilibrium between one full vessel and one empty. This is how we share sorrow and ease our grief. My writing the essay later formed the bond with the radio audience which allowed me to share the sorrow with some of the listeners.

Thus do we spread sorrow out among us and make it not only bearable but palatable for each of us. The young man in the park has become one of my fondest memories from all my time in Europe. Sorrow is like salt. In the doses that we can handle, it heightens our sense of life's beauty.

※ ※

As a boy, I used to wish that my life would never become mundane. Not having experienced great hardship or suffering, I romanticized the ideal life as a series of peaks and valleys. The greater one fell into sadness and suffering, the higher one could rise to see (and create) beauty. I ached to witness great beauty. To feel something of life's heights and depths. It was a bohemian view of life, but I held fast to it.

In the years that we have lived with Elie's terminal illness, I have often sensed in other people the belief that it would be better if Elie were to die sooner rather than later. It always remains unspoken, but the way they frame their thoughts or prognosticate our future, I feel certain that they assume God's blessing to us would be for Elie to die soon and without pain. For whatever reason, these people feel she is a hardship, that it would make our lives easier or steadier if she were gone, that it would strengthen our marriage by giving us more time together, less stress. The person who thinks this evinces a great show of sympathy for us. They offer to help, but seldom do. They say things like, "I only wish that I could do something to ease your pain." Their expressions virtually drip with empathy for my sadness.

But these people are fools. I was right when I was a boy. Suffering is a gift. Thoreau said, "The mass of men lead lives of quiet desperation." I now know the desperation comes not because men suffer from loss or grief, but precisely because they are afraid to suffer and so fear to try anything. Suffering wakes us from the torpor that leads to desperation. Grief makes us aware enough to experience beauty and joy.

Phillip Keller writes, "As Christians we will sooner or later discover that it is in the valleys of our lives that we find refreshment from God Himself. It is not until we have walked with Him through some very deep troubles that we discover He can lead us to find our refreshment in Him right there in the midst of our difficulty."

So many people seem to set as a life goal the desire to avoid any great hardship, any suffering, any grief. I remember a trip with my parents on their friend's sailboat. We left a Long Island port near New York and sailed east past the Great Peconic Bay, then along the coast to Block Island. The entire trip there, we were becalmed and so had to motor. It took three days. For half of the crew it was a calm, pleasant journey—and just what they desired.

On the trip back, we set out in a driving easterly wind and reached all of the way back in one day, finally ending with three reefs in the mainsail and the wind blowing 40 knots. The rollers in Long Island Sound were eight to ten feet high and looked always as if they would swamp the boat until the stern lifted and yawed over them. Every now and then a rogue wave would break green water over the rails. I remember clearly looking at my mother who sat in the cockpit, knuckles white with fear and seasickness and laughing at myself because I had never felt so invigorated in my life.

It strikes me as a good metaphor for the two approaches to life. To experience such invigoration, we have to be willing to give up the safe and the steady. Storm clouds produce the most beautiful landscapes. But we have to be willing to endure the storm.

My children are the greatest gifts I have known, but Elie is particularly special. She makes my life far richer, more contemplative, and full of joy than it ever would have been without her. She is a beloved—even essential—addition to our home and will be as long as she is with us. Elie has given me an awareness of suffering's noble beauty, but this awareness is bought at the price of my own child's certain death. It is not possible to convey this sense to someone who has not experienced it, but I am filled with the certainty that this suffering is a gift from God.

As I recall my boyhood prayer, I realize that it was answered. In my stubborn optimism toward life, I am reminded of lines from a favorite Frost poem:

> ...I do not see why I should e're turn back
> Or those should not set forth upon my track
> To overtake me, who should miss me here
> And long to know if still I held them dear.
> They would not find me changed from him they knew —
> Only more sure of all I thought was true.

༄ ༄

The day following Elie's first prognosis, we walked through the courtyard at C.S. Mott hospital, Elie in a borrowed stroller, Liz and I pushing her. My parents followed behind. It was a beautiful, spring day in Ann Arbor. Elie was dressed in a hospital gown and a pink beret pulled down over her ears. The courtyard was lined with crabapple trees in full flower, delicate pink and white blossoms dropping petals on the grass. Patients and staff sat along the low walls and on the benches, soaking up the warmth and gentle fragrance of spring, drinking coffee, relaxing in small groups.

Liz and I could not stop staring at Elie. It was as if each look was the last. The first shock of a prognosis of a terminal disease leads one to prepare for more sudden shocks. We both wondered if she would die that afternoon, or that night, or next week. All we could do was look at her, trying to so capture her image in our minds so that we could hold it there forever if we lost her suddenly.

And we cried. We held her in the sunshine and laughed at her gurgling, even as tears rolled down our cheeks. She was totally unconcerned. Having no aspirations, she had no fears. Without language, her future was indefinable. Her innocence was striking, particularly in light of the hard fate she had been given.

The doctors had offered us a number of options, and we had to discuss each that afternoon. The surgeon suggested a biopsy to see if the tumor was, in fact, malignant. She offered us another option of chemotherapy to try and treat the tumor, but she held out little optimism for this. The former she offered not necessarily for Elie's benefit but more in the cause of science. She said that if it were her child, she would want to know. All of the doctors gave us the clear impression that it did not make much sense to treat Elie because the prognosis was so bleak no matter what.

Even without speaking, Liz and I were remarkably attuned and our immediate decision was finalized in a matter of a few moments and a few words: we would do nothing that would cause her pain, we wanted Elie to be as comfortable as possible, we did not want to use treatment or surgery to prolong life solely for the sake of prolonging life. We both felt that the quality of life was the critical aspect, not the length. Our agreement was remarkable because we had never discussed this openly. It had never occurred to us to talk about dying, cancer, tumors, treatments. Yet we were absolutely united in our resolve. On so many small things, Liz and I disagree, but on this most important point we were aligned. We would care for and love our daughter for as long as we had her. Liz and I vowed that Elie would be held and loved by us and her extended family as long as she lived. To this day, the single-mindedness with which we have remained true to this pledge I still find hard to comprehend—a grace given to us in our need.

That afternoon's decision to love her was more than just a decision about Elie. It was also a decision about God. We both consciously and openly acknowledged that we had no way to explain or understand these cruel events. Our first born would die: that was all we knew. Our obligation was clear, however. We would take care of her to the best of our ability as long as she remained with us. The rest we left with God, the reason for the tumor, the mystery of one child being taken when so many others around us were healthy. We continued to pray for a miracle, but we accepted that afternoon that she would die. Love for Elie was our sole and single-minded purpose.

Elizabeth Kübler-Ross writes in *On Death and Dying* that the stages of reaction to crisis or death are denial, anger, bargaining, despair, and finally acceptance. In some strange way, by placing the love for our child above all else we skipped a number of these steps. Often the initial reaction to someone's death is, "Why did this happen to me," implying that the death of someone else is somehow also a death of part of ourselves. Yet when it happens to a child, the instinctive reaction as parents is to think of the child—not ourselves. I do not think we were ever angry. We never asked why this would happen to us. Our prayers by the bedside may have been bargaining—we both asked that God not take her away soon, that he let her have a while longer, and Liz particularly asked that we have her until we had another child so that we would never be childless from her death—but we never felt despair for her death. Late that night we ordered pizza and, with Elie being passed from lap to lap, many of us were playing poker on the floor and laughing. Nurses and doctors entering the room that evening, with purposefully sad faces found us seated around a towel on the floor with a pile of poker chips in the middle and a half-naked Elie bouncing on a grandparent's lap.

Some may argue that this was a part of denial, but I really think it was a sudden, transforming acceptance. We would cry still many times, feel sudden, wrenching pain. Such was natural with the knowledge of

Elie's coming death. But Liz summed it up later that night when she said, "I feel better knowing that we will take care of her and that she will be loved and comforted for as long as she lives. I just want to take her home and be with family. I want to rock her when she dies. And when she dies, she'll go straight from my arms to God's."

CHAPTER 5
A Picture

From the first few weeks of her life, our relatives have all commented how much Elie looks like me. We have the same hair, the same shape to our faces, the same eyes—though a different color. We are a father and daughter with a remarkable, physical resemblance. And I have always sensed that the physical somehow manifests the deeper spiritual bond we share. She is my daughter. She is a part of me. I know before anyone else, even her mother, what she wants or needs. I know when she is too cold. I know when she is hungry. I know when she will wake. Even when she has been in one of her deepest sleeps, I can sense if she will wake as I walk past. She knows I am there, and she calls me when she needs me.

In the wee hours, when she has lain stiff in the nurse's arms since midnight and even Liz cannot put her to sleep, I will take her in my lap, hold her hand in mine, wrap the blanket around her and she will soften slowly, then bat her eyelids heavily, and within moments drift off into a deep sleep. She was waiting for me to come to her, but had no way of telling the nurse or Liz other than by stiffening out.

When I return after work, she is often in her chair. I drop my bag and kiss her on the cheek and say, "Lift your hand to greet me." Her body stiffens slightly, she tenses her face and groans, and then her hand comes up in what appears to be almost a voluntary motion. I know it is probably not voluntary though she does this for no one else. She hears me at least.

Our newborn son is obviously his mother's; they are connected. I love him. I love to hold him, carry him in my arms, change him on the table while he stares at the mobile above his head and laughs. But he is definitely his mother's child. Elie is mine. I think God made that bond so strong, so seemingly telepathic, because He knew Elie would need it. She was given no way to communicate by normal means, so she had to have someone who could understand her through extra-ordinary means.

I wonder sometimes if this almost telepathic bond can be developed or if it is innate. I tend to think it is the latter, but it grows as we nurture our love for the child. Most often only mother and child have it, perhaps strengthened through the power of breast feeding and nature. But Elie and I have it. We are linked, and the link is like an imperceptible spiritual nerve that connects us. It was always there, but as love grows and becomes more complex, so grows the complexity of the connection and the messages it can carry. At some point, speech becomes unnecessary, and understanding travels back and forth directly.

In the months to come, we asked much of God. We asked for healing, we asked for support, we asked for time—always we asked for time. There was so much to ask for and we were so intent on asking, that I wonder now if we ever thought to thank Him for what He had already given us. A child is a gift. This gift of life is precious. But to be given a child of incomparable beauty, a child whose outward appearance manifests the purity of her inner self, was more than a parent could ask. Liz and I have lived with an angel in our house for three years. That is something for which to give thanks.

And could I really expect to hold onto that beauty forever? The complexity of life is incredible, as is the frailty of human existence. We cling to our belief in the permanence of all that surrounds us, we pray for permanence, and yet all permanence is illusion. Death and the sense of loss we feel comes from the *mistaken belief that permanence is possible. At each moment, though, events occur to forever change the structure of the universe as it relates to us. Herodotus said all things are in flux. Elie's beauty cannot last forever. And yet God has retained her childish purity. With that comes beauty. And I cannot ask her to be always this way, nor should I. The real beauty is the love that underlies her existence, whether physical beauty dies or not.*

◈ ◈

There is another aspect of beauty which is more difficult to describe and yet no less important than the physical. That is the beauty born of suffering—a piquant, lovely, fragile form of beauty. Elie wears it at the corners of her eyes and the swollen skin around her joints. This beauty is not always attractive, but it is always compelling. Like the nearly hidden scar that graces her hairline from her widow's peak to her earlobe, it becomes an outward sign of her willingness to endure adversity. There is a great beauty hidden in steadfastness.

Elie's suffering and endurance have given her a rare aura in this world. She is a child who can hardly communicate, who depends on others to know and meet her needs, who has little to look forward to with joy but the moments of comfort provided by her parents and nurses. I ask myself often what if she is only physically disabled but her mind still functions? What if she has dreams and hopes? What if she is trying to communicate but cannot? As a parent, it is terrible to imagine these things because they may be true and we would never know it. Yet for her, trapped inside a strong but non-functional body, to endure takes heroism and love. The love comes from us, but the heroism is all hers. And there is beauty in that as well.

I bathed Elie myself tonight. I held her head between two hands and let her body float in the soothing water. She slept until the water cooled, then woke and smacked her lips together softly. If I shut my eyes it was almost like waves lapping at the shore. As I lifted her from the bath, she pulled her legs up and curled into fetal position, her arms across her chest and clenched. I set her on the warmed towels and began to rub her scalp to dry it. She scrunched up her face when the towel touched her lips. I drew it away. I dried around her waist, between her legs, under her arms, her feet, her hands, in her ears. She suffered through everything, making hardly a sound. As I lifted her from the bathmat and cradled her naked into my chest, she sighed. A soft intake of breath and then... a relaxation. Relief, love, comfort. It all comes out in that barely audible sigh. She does this often for me. It remains one of the most beautiful sounds I have ever known.

❧ ☙

It is important to picture Elie because in large part her presence is what captivated people and drew them to her and us. Though diminutive and powerless, the purity of her beauty and her obvious frailty radiated in a way that unlocks the human heart. We reached out to her, in part because of the way suffering shaped her lovely features, but largely for the loveliness itself. Her beauty caused many strangers to approach our family, if for no other reason than to see her more closely.

We were once stuck in O'Hare airport, waiting for a flight home after a wedding. The flights were all delayed due to fog and our departure was put back from 8 pm until 11:55. The airport was cool and Elie is always cold, so I was holding her seated in my lap as she slept with a coat wrapped over her legs and stomach. A couple sitting in the chairs opposite us kept looking at her. They were not being impolite. They just kept looking our way.

About an hour later the man was standing in front of me. He held two airline blankets in his hand. "I searched around and finally found these at a gate near the end of the terminal," he said. "We thought it would help keep your daughter warm."

"She's a beautiful girl," his wife said, across the row of seats.

We thanked them and they departed, having never even exchanged any names other than Elie's. For her first five years, Elie looked completely normal when she slept, and I do not think they ever knew she was handicapped. They were simply acting out of kindness and responding to her loveliness.

※ ※

When I look back at the photos we have of Elie as a young infant, I am struck by two things. First, I am surprised by how young she looks, how little hair she had, how round and babyish her features are. But second, I am amazed by her angelic grace. It is difficult to describe a child's features, and so I can only begin by saying that even when she was very young, we would often comment that she looked like one of the cherubim from a high Renaissance painting.

Her hair was strawberry blond with a slight wave in it. Liz liked to leave it long over Elie's forehead, and we'd blow it back from her face when we held her. It most often smelled of Johnson's Baby Shampoo and fresh straw; the bath was one of her few pleasures, warming her and allowing her to relax completely and float off to sleep for 20 minutes, her knees and hands bobbing above the surface as we cradled her head in one arm over the edge of the tub.

Elie's eyes were greenish-hazel streaked through with yellow. She had the longest, darkest eyelashes I have ever seen. Her eyelashes were probably the feature most often noticed, particularly by women. She had a small, rosebud mouth that slumped open when in a deep sleep. Her open mouth let us know she was sleeping soundly enough to put her to bed without waking her and having to start the process all over again, which can take hours of rocking. Her teeth came in slowly, and only halfway, as if lack of use and chewing prevented them from emerging fully. This gave her the look of a smaller child. It also caused one of her biggest discomforts, tender gums and a very sensitive mouth, a problem that only increased over time.

At three, her skin was as soft as a newborn's and had a light down toward the back of her jawline. When she was warm, had a fever, or was teething, her cheeks blazed crimson like a rose on cream-colored silk. When she dropped into one of her deep sleeps, her cheeks lost their color making her face look pallid, as if foreshadowing death.

Her primary care doctor near our home in Michigan, a wonderful, caring young German-born man named Bernd Holler, had a colleague whose daughter died of a brain tumor. As the neurosurgeon in Ann Arbor had predicted for us, this poor child's head grew increasingly large with the pressure created by a rapidly expanding tumor. Since she was young and her cranium was still malleable, her head simply grew until it was nearly the size of a small watermelon. It must have been quite horrifying because I remember Liz, Elie and I dropped in once to see some other friends who were also colleagues of Bernd's. The husband, a surgeon, met us at the door and invited us to wait in the living room for his wife, who would return momentarily. After a short wait, we heard her come in and, just outside the door, she whispered urgently to her husband, "What does she look like?"

"Normal," he replied in the same whisper. "Quite beautiful, in fact."

As she got a bit older, the steroid treatment Elie required combined with her lack of activity caused her at times to grow quite moon-faced and chubby. She retained her baby fat so that her knuckles were mere indents and her fingers thick. She had a round belly that hung over her diaper, but her legs were thin and, except for the inward turning feet caused by her spasticity, looked very normal.

I often wonder what she would look like if she could have walked across the room to me. She would teeter uneasily, reaching out to steady herself on the coffee table. She would step forward, smiling. She would set one foot forward and then lunge toward me with three simple steps. I have seen it in dreams and woken knowing I had seen her walk, but it is one of those simple pleasures which most parents take for granted and I will never know.

∽ ∾

Elie had an extraordinary wardrobe, and Liz made an effort to see that Elie was dressed well every morning. She was changed immediately if she threw up or wet herself, and always had warm pajamas and socks at night.

There were two dresses in particular that meant the most to me. One was a simple, blue tartan dress made of light cotton with a matching beret and a red ribbon. My parents gave it to Elie for her second Christmas and, sometime in the course of that week, someone snapped a photo of her face in which, by some small miracle, she appears to be looking directly at the camera. She has a small, melancholy pout and her eyes are deep and dark. I know it is illusory, but as I stare at that photo, I get a feeling that I have never gotten—that she is looking at me and that she understands enough to be a little sad.

The second dress was a very fancy English dress purchased from a New York boutique to celebrate Elie's first birthday. At eight months, we thought she would not have a first birthday. When it came around, we invited more than 50 friends to Liz's family home, where we were staying with Elie, had games and presents for the kids, dressed Elie in this yellow taffeta dress with petticoats and celebrated her being with us. It was both a happy and sad event because Elie was unconscious for most of the party, but the joy that it brought us to be able to choose a party dress for her birthday was indelible.

I am most accustomed to seeing Elie, however, in one of her three or four sleepers. Red, green, yellow, aqua—each made of warm, terry cloth with a Winnie-the-Pooh motif above the breast—they have become so worn from washing that the cotton has begun to pill. Still, we dressed her in them every evening with a pair of socks underneath and a pair of booties over. We would zip them up and snap the button at the throat. We would lay a hot water bottle across her legs, and she was ready to fall asleep on the couch, rocked gently by one of us or the nurse.

It would seem easy to neglect the appearance of a child who knows no better, who seldom goes out, who will never benefit from this special care other than in the sense that it is a way of showing love, soaked up as readily as we could give it. But when the child is your own, you soon realize that rather than neglect, you must take special pains to care for the child that cannot care for itself. Christy Brown, in *My Left Foot,* wrote of his own mother's attitude to his cerebral palsy:

> *She refused to accept this truth, the inevitable truth—as it then seemed—that I was beyond cure, beyond saving, even beyond hope... Finding that the doctors could not help telling her... to forget I was a human creature, rather to regard me as just something to be fed and washed and then put away again, mother decided there and then to take matters into her own hands. I was her child, and therefore part of the family. No matter how dull and incapable I might grow up to be, she was determined to treat me on the same plane as the others, and not as the 'queer one' in the back room who was never spoken of when there were visitors present.... Mother wasn't content just to say that I was not an idiot, she set out to prove it, not because of any rigid sense of duty, but out of love. That is why she was so successful.*

CHAPTER 6

Reconciliation

On Sunday, after our time in the Ann Arbor hospital, I put Liz on a plane and she flew with Elie to her home in New York. It was Mothers Day, May 8, and we had spent four days in the hospital.

My father and I returned north to Cedarville by car to pack up clothes and other items that I could bring with me when I followed a few days later. There was a real sense of reconciliation and acceptance after leaving Ann Arbor and the hospital, though it did not make the nights alone any easier. I lay in the bed after hanging up with Liz each night and cried for hours, trying to remain quiet enough that my father, who was sleeping in the adjacent room, could not hear me. But an early form of acceptance did come, mainly because of the mission we had set ourselves, that we would make Elie's remaining days with us as comfortable and joyful as possible. We wanted her to be in the midst of a big family who would love and hold her, and we would devote ourselves to her comforts.

Liz, I think, even more than me found a great sense of relief that our tragedy and our decisions were behind us. By accepting that Elie would die, it became easier to fill her life with love. I knew that surrounded by her brothers and sisters, her parents, other relatives and friends, Liz could really accomplish the task. I knew there was laughter in that house, and Elie would be encircled by people who were full of joy.

It was different for me from the beginning. While I closed the house, packed our bags, set up for a long-term leave from work, I had a taste of what was to come. I remember listening by phone to the family around the table a thousand miles away, the laughter, hearing Liz's voice, most of all hearing Elie's gurgles and coos. My daughter was making sounds that I knew were coming from a mouth half-paralyzed. I begged Liz not to put me on speaker phone because I could never hear that without breaking down. I would just listen, slumped back in my study chair, weeping silently for thirty minutes. Just listen to Liz and try to imagine Elie and the smile she might be wearing. The distance—even for a short time, when time was filled with such uncertainty—filled my part of our mission with anguish.

Yet early on, I only had a vague suspicion of the sadness that distance would cause. At this point, we were sure her remaining life would be short. The Ann Arbor doctors had told us so, and our own instinct confirmed it. Already this tumor had affected her motor skills, had paralyzed her arm. Things seemed to be moving quickly, and our time was short. We would all be together in Port Washington, we would take long walks with her in the stroller, read to her and each other, kiss her, and—when the time came—let her go.

Looking back I am surprised by the quickness of our acceptance. It was due in part to innocence. We knew nothing of brain tumors or a child dying. Ignorance and an innocence of the pain that grief brings made it possible for us to find peace. If we had to face it again, with years of experience behind us, it might be harder to move toward acceptance so quickly. Liz has often said that if she knew then what she knows now, she could not have survived Elie's illness. Our innocence allowed us to suspend disbelief and anger.

More than innocence, however, our acceptance was a direct acknowledgment of faith. We accepted tragedy because we acknowledged immediately and independently that there were parts of this tragedy we could not control. For Liz, it was God's plan. For me, it was a course of events beyond my control or understanding. If I could not control this course of events, then I must accept it. Like Liz, in a roundabout way I was also acknowledging a divine power. Elie had a brain tumor and it would kill her. We could not change that. Only God could. The sole option within our power was to control the way we reacted to it. The reaction that we both chose was one of love.

More than the speed of our acceptance, though, I am amazed by the unanimity of it. I can imagine that this point of acceptance is so often the grit that wears down the emotional cogs of a loving marriage. We must all, when facing tragedy, at some point accept and move on. But individuals have their own ways of moving toward that acceptance. A couple that moves along different paths and at different speeds toward acceptance could easily be torn apart. Many are. I read in one book on grieving that 80% of marriages in which a child dies end in divorce. Grieving and the need to accept the heavy burden of loss, when they occur separately and at different rates, ruin two people's compatibility. A husband, who has accepted, cannot live with and relate to a wife who has not yet accepted, or vice-versa.

For us, though, acceptance was immediate. We never talked about it, we never argued. We just accepted. And both our marriage and our ability to help with the problems to come were strengthened.

I am often touched by the saying that God always answers our prayers but he answers them in unexpected ways. Perhaps as we knelt against the bed praying that our daughter would be healed, we ourselves were touched by the healing grace of God. Perhaps it descended in the form of acceptance. I have no other way to explain how three hours after finding out the worst news a parent can hear, we were all seated on the floor of the hospital laughing, playing cards, and eating pizza. This healing for us may have been God's means to provide the security and love that we intended toward Elie. Our love for Elie was part of our love for each other. Perhaps God moved to protect the one and aid the other.

I say perhaps because I have difficulty writing convincingly about something I do not understand. This is and is not a story about faith. 'Perhaps' is my reflexive conditional when it comes to God. I believe, yet I do not understand. I have faith, yet I wonder if He manages the minutiae of small events. I can only say that despite our different beliefs about religion and God, Liz and I made the exact same decision at the same moment, both being given equal voice in determining the course of events. Neither of us influenced the other, nor did we speak about it other than to confirm our decision.

Perhaps this decision—and I say perhaps consciously—was a work of grace.

⋘ ⋙

The few days that my father and I spent in Cedarville closing up the house also gave me the first intimation of how an entire town could close ranks to help one of its members. It was a revelation that has stayed with me and changed my perspective of the world and my relation to community.

In those first days we had dinner brought to us each night. Acquaintances dropped by to check on me, folks I had met a few times but with whom I had very little contact. Members of other churches called to offer help or meals.

Having never been through a tragedy, I did not know how to react. At times, it felt as if people were merely satisfying their own curiosity, even prying. Prior to this moment, I was unaware of how people reach out to each other and, though I am sure it happened often, I simply did not hear or see it. When the priest called during Mass for a special prayer on behalf of some ill member of the community, I was usually tuned out. I did not know them. I did not know their illness. I could not sympathize.

But a strong community is like a hive of bees. Those calls, the unannounced visits by pastors or elders from other churches, the casual references in conversation at the bank or supermarket, they were a form of reconnaissance by the community scouts. And those visits would set in motion a whole network of activities depending on the report and the sense of need expressed by the scouts. I have seen it now many times since for other members of the community, this coming together of people. People acting in unison without any preconceived plan, moved by some common spirit and a sense of obligation toward each other.

At this early point, however, I did not realize how much we would depend on the community of friends and supporters. I may have been fairly short with those who called on us in Cedarville, feeling often as if it were an invasion of my privacy. At that point, all I wanted was to follow Liz and Elie to New York.

Aside from packing clothes and closing the house, an important reason for returning to Cedarville was to settle with my company the details of an extended leave of absence. We came to Michigan because of an opportunity I had to work for The Nature Conservancy. It was a fun and challenging job, but as I was the point person in the community, it required my constant involvement. Our state headquarters was 300 miles away; the primary focus of that office was on the project I directed. We were investing millions of dollars in the area, and my leave would take away the only representative of the organization in the community at a critical point in the evolution of the project.

And yet my colleagues never wavered in their willingness to accommodate my needs. The words spoken first and often were, "Take as long as you need." Beyond the statutory leave, they found ways again and again to allow me to spend time with my family, to pick up among themselves pieces of the work I was supposed to be doing. They kept the project going, and they allowed me to focus on my own more pressing needs. Later, after our situation with Elie had changed, the circumstances of my leave became more difficult. But they stood by me throughout, even allowing me to work part-time as much as I could from an apartment in New York City.

These blessings, a caring community and understanding employer, were critical to our well being. In dealing with tragedy, one needs to feel some sense of security wherever possible. A catastrophe turns the world literally on end for the victim; we piece the world back together little by little as we find individual items with which we feel secure. Our family, our home, our friends, our colleagues, our church, our community. These are the individuals and institutions that bless and sustain us through loss.

∼∽

I left by plane with my father on a Wednesday. We flew together to LaGuardia, where he would catch a shuttle to the city and where I was to be met by my in-laws. His business would bring him to New York for extended stays over the next few months, sometimes with my mother, living out of a Park Avenue hotel and negotiating around-the-clock for days at a time. Every once in a while, though, he would steal away for a few hours to visit us on Long Island or, when we were settled at a hospital in the lower East Side, in the city itself.

Liz's youngest brother, John, met us at the baggage claim. Her father was waiting with the car just outside. The sun was shining and it was one of those brisk, blue mornings that break on New York almost by surprise. Business travelers moved across the sidewalk toward cabs or the various shuttle buses. Cars waiting along the curb picked up passengers and drove off quickly. I had the feeling that would recur time after time that everyone else's life was moving along, the world was still going, but mine had come to a standstill. The rear of the station wagon swung open. I loaded my bags in the back, hugged my father goodbye, and drove off for Port Washington.

With a dying child, time seems to slow. There is a feeling of waiting—not anticipation—just waiting. Or maybe time doesn't slow so much as the many things that clutter our lives drop away and we are left with just one thing that occupies us completely. As the multitude of cares and concerns vanish, we suddenly feel a bit empty, in limbo. Nothing except the dying child has any meaning, nothing really matters, and the child's death is going to happen in the future, at some undefined time and place. Our lives become simply a period of waiting for that death.

That is what I kept thinking as I watched the exit signs tick by on the Long Island Expressway. Familiar signs: Utopia Parkway, Cross Island, Van Wyck, Exit 29, 30, Great Neck, Searingtown Road. Each slipped by, luminous green signs marking a passing moment, with our exit off in the future. Elie's moment some time away, yet ineluctable.

There is a blankness in this waiting. Or perhaps it is a blackness. It was filled for me to some extent by my resolve to comfort my daughter, but that only filled it partially. I was not able to do much for Elie at this point. In many ways, she was a normal girl still. Unconscious of her growing disability, unconcerned by it. She was happy, Liz was happy, and there was nothing for me to do.

If this time had lasted longer, I think it would have become more difficult. A terminal illness makes everyone surrounding the illness feel helpless anyway. But added to that is the sense of aimlessness, of waiting. I had no job to do, a child who was happy, I was out of my own home, my only task to comfort Liz when, as often happened to both of us—usually in the privacy of a bedroom—she was overcome by a wave of anguish.

An early scene in *A Tale of Two Cities* describes the father of the heroine imprisoned in the Bastille. Deprived of his wits by a long and unexplained prison sentence, he becomes a hollow man, only his work tools and the shoes that he mends of any importance to him at all. His hands, in a sense, provide the escape that his mind craves, and he is consumed by the repetitive work of a cobbler. Even after he has been freed, Manon cannot put down his tools. The work of his hands has been the only thing that keeps him sane and alive.

Dickens was a master of capturing the human condition, and this characterization in one of my favorite works has always stayed with me. Because of Elie, I found out why. Our work, no matter what form it takes, is something that gives us continuity and dignity. For the year since Elie was born, I had been fixing up our house. I had rebuilt the chimney, put in a woodstove, begun to rewire the house, insulated the attic. On my list was replacing the bathroom and fitting a skylight, gutting and rebuilding the kitchen, putting up new walls in the entry and a beam in the living room. I had worked during almost all of my free time. Leisure, for me, was doing something productive, making the house more comfortable for my family. The lack of work for me, the endless sitting on couches, talking to relatives, thinking about my own problems, was very difficult. Later, when Elie's situation changed, the lack of work would become unbearable and I, like Manon, would turn to my hands to keep me sane. For now, though, I was simply waiting. We were all waiting.

Liz was at church in Port Washington with her father and Elie the day before I was scheduled to return. Liz had mentioned one evening on the phone that it would have been nice to take Elie to Lourdes and bathe her in the waters that had caused miracles for the hopeless in the past.

When Liz and I were living at Oxford, Liz joined a group of Catholic pilgrims who traveled to Lourdes to volunteer in the baths as helpers for the sick. The group spent a week there, and Liz said at the time it was the most rewarding work she had ever done.

She dismissed her idea as being impossible though, largely because our time was short and home was a safe place to stay. I thought a lot about it after that phone call. Being so far away made me want to do something for them, and I decided that we would go to Lourdes. I told my father about my plan, and I reasoned that it would be a great comfort to Liz. I told him I thought it was something she needed. I did not say that I wanted to go because I hoped desperately for a miracle to cure my daughter. I did not tell him that I read night after night the same story from the Bible about the father who searches for Jesus and begs him to come quickly because his daughter is dying, and Jesus saves the child. I hoped beyond hope that I could be that man and see my daughter cured, but I was afraid to admit the solitary desperation of my longing to my father or the real purpose beyond my resolve to get my family to Lourdes.

At church that day, the priest and congregation prayed a special intention for Elie, and afterwards many of the friends and acquaintances of the Russos stopped to talk and inquire what was wrong with their granddaughter. One woman, on hearing of the brain tumor, pulled Frank aside and told him that she had had a dream about a little girl with a brain tumor just the night before. She was from out of town visiting her son, whom the Russos knew, but they had never met her before. She explained that in the dream she saw Elie's face and then she saw a bright light and Jesus bending down to cup Elie's head in His hands. She had known it was a child with a brain tumor and had even remarked about the dream to her son that morning.

"I think it means that she will be all right," the woman told Frank before leaving.

Another woman at the same Mass suggested the name of a doctor at NYU Hospital. Liz explained as politely as she could that Elie's case was inoperable and we were simply trying to make her as comfortable as possible. "I understand," the woman said, "but I've written his name down on a piece of paper for you just in case you want to see him later. They call him the 'miracle doctor' because he treats tumors that no one else can." Liz put the piece of paper in her wallet and left.

When I arrived at the house, Frank was explaining that a secretary at his office had suggested we go see another doctor, a specialist, to get a second opinion. He explained that she knew someone with a brain tumor and had gotten the name of the doctor. Frank told me, and I tried to explain that we had made our decision and he should respect that. "If it is inoperable, Frank," I said as patiently as possible, "I am not going to some doctor who will talk me into doing chemo that will make her miserable. She's a happy child." I wanted her to stay that way.

One of the first jobs on my list, however, was to find a pediatrician in Port Washington who could help us and prescribe any pain medications or morphine Elie might need. I wanted to get things set up right away. The father of Liz's best friend was an ophthalmologist. We called him and he suggested a doctor in Manhasset. I made an appointment for the following day.

It was a tremendous relief to be back with Liz and Elie at last. I had only been away a few days, but those days were torturous. I realized just how hard they had been when I finally pulled up to the house and Liz met me in the driveway, holding my beautiful daughter in her arms. Elie's face lit up when I stepped out of the car, and I hugged her as tightly as I could. Her mouth still sagged, but it did not seem as bad as it had. She laughed when I nuzzled her neck. The paralysis in her arm was still evident.

"I'm taking you to Lourdes," I told Liz as we stood in the driveway.

"What?" she said.

"I think we should go," I said.

"Do you think we can?" I could see a sudden flush of happiness in Liz's face. Her cheeks had been drawn and pale, but they were suffused with a warm blush at the thought. "Could we do it?" she said again.

"We'll find a way," I answered, and I felt better than I had felt in two weeks. We were at last doing something for Elie, and I was doing something for Liz. We needed something to look forward to, some ray of hope. Lourdes was it. That night we talked for a long time. Liz told me about the woman and her dream. We held our sleeping daughter between us. We were filled with hope.

<hr />

The following morning, we drove to Manhasset to see the doctor. It was a short wait in a very clean office, and then the doctor came in. He was young and robust. His hair was dark with a cowlick of grey above one temple and a very warm smile. He listened to our explanation of the past two weeks and the diagnosis at Ann Arbor, then he turned in his seat and reached for the phone.

"I want you to see a colleague of mine," he told us. "It is always good to seek a second opinion, but in a case like this, it is critical."

I was reluctant. Our decision was made, and I was afraid of false hope or worse.

"You can always ignore his advice if you don't think it is right," the doctor said. "But he is the best of the best. I think you should see him as soon as possible."

"How quickly could he see us," Liz asked. She smiled, "We're taking Elie to Lourdes soon."

"Quickly, I think," he answered as he dialed a number. "I was chief resident in pediatrics for his floor. I dealt with a lot of his cases. He'll see you if he can." Ten minutes later, we had an appointment for the following afternoon. "Come back once you've seen Fred and we can talk about your options again," the doctor said as he saw us to the door.

I took the address and thanked him. Liz and I both left feeling a little more depressed. "I thought it would be easier now that we have decided what to do for Elie," she said.

I agreed with her. "But we can always ignore the advice if we don't like it," I repeated. "We're not doing anything you and I don't believe in."

That night at the dinner table, Liz's mother Bette told us about a woman in her religious group who had told her about a doctor at NYU that was famous for saving kids with brain tumors. "His name is Fred Epstein," Bette said off-handedly.

"WHAT?" exclaimed Frank, who was usually dramatic about coincidences. "That was the name of the doctor my secretary recommended to me yesterday at work. What a coincidence! Maybe you should go see him."

"We're seeing him tomorrow afternoon," I said quietly. "Dr. Rossi gave us his name as well. He set up the appointment for us." I was determined that I was not going to start clutching at any flimsy excuse for hope and I would not be talked into doing something against my better judgment.

Frank was persistent. "Do you realize what the likelihood is of three different people all giving you the name of the same doctor within 24 hours of each other. Maybe this is the miracle we've been praying for."

I was frustrated. "Look," I said, "It's a malignant tumor. It's the size of a golfball. It's growing fast. It's in the middle of the brain. Please don't act like a great doctor could just make all of this go away."

The table was very quiet. Liz got up and left the kitchen. I felt badly about getting angry at the people around me. "I didn't mean to raise my voice," I said. "It's just that I hate to have false hopes."

Liz returned to the table holding a little piece of paper. "A woman in church gave the name of a doctor to me as well," she said. "She called him 'the miracle doctor.' His name is Fred Epstein."

There was absolute quiet. Liz was smiling, then Frank spoke. "That's five different people all recommending the same doctor in two days. Do you know what the likelihood of that is? I'd say 200,000 to 1. Maybe Epstein can do something. Maybe this is the miracle we have been praying for."

The table began chattering wildly. There was such a need for hope in our family. The miracle for us was a flash of light and a quick fix, not something slower and more life changing. We wanted a healthy child so badly and we were so debilitated by the fear of the tumor, that at the time the idea of a miracle which included the tumor and did not vanquish it never entered our minds. I was no exception, and though I hoped for a cure, I could only say, "We'll see." I felt as if these shiftless hopes could only disturb our equanimity. I was sure that medical science could do nothing for us. Lourdes was our only hope. The hope offered by medical science seemed like a trap.

Above all else I feared being talked into a course of action that would lead to my daughter lying strapped to a hospital bed for two years with tubes coming out of her body, totally helpless, a vegetable. I would let her go before I would risk that. There was no joy in life lived in a hospital bed, no love in treatments and tubes and a slow withering. It was my own greatest fear, and I would not be talked into allowing it.

CHAPTER 7
A Day in the Life

I slept in late this morning. I'm only three and a half so I don't know how to tell time, but the sun was already coming through the window and shining on my face when I finally woke up. The sun is one of my favorite things; I can't see it, but I can feel warmth on my face and it heats my skin up in a different way than other things. Not just on the surface but down underneath, like the inside of my cheeks was getting warm as well.

Beth was here when I woke up, and she moved me down to a blanket on the floor so that I could have my whole body in the sun. Beth has a big lap. I just sink into her lap and lean my head against her, and it's very easy to fall asleep. Sometimes they don't want me to sleep, so they put me on the floor and make me do exercises.

I like some of the exercises because my legs are sore from lying a certain way for a long time. The only part I don't like is when they put me on my tummy. I get scared because I can't turn my head and my nose gets pressed into the blanket. Beth rubs my back and sometimes I can push up.

I smelled my Mommy a few times this morning, but I think I was still sleeping and just dreamed it maybe. She comes out to check on me a lot during the night. When I'm awake, Mommy likes to pick me up and kiss my cheeks, and I like that too. Most of the time, I can't do anything to let her know I like it, but every once in a while when I'm thinking about how much I like being picked up by Mommy, all of the sudden a noise comes out. She says I'm sighing.

Our house is small. I can tell because no matter where Mommy goes, I can hear her. She talks a lot and is usually happy. I wish I could say things back to her, but nothing comes out—except for sighs.

I live on the couch. We have a wood stove that Daddy fills with logs each day. It keeps me warm. I don't know why, but my hands and feet are really cold sometimes. Usually they are cold when I wake up, so someone puts me on the carpet and rubs my legs, which they say are thin and beautiful, and my hands, which they say are pudgy and fat, to warm them up.

Beth massages me, then she makes me do work. It's very hard and hurts me a little. I have to sit straight up and lift my arms over my head. I can't do that myself, so Beth cradles me between her legs and holds my arms up for me. I lower them down again myself, sometimes one more than the other. I never really know what's going to happen until it's happened.

After we're finished on the floor, I go straight to my standing table. They strap my legs to it, then turn the handle and slowly raise me up so that I'm standing. They say it's good to have weight on my bones, but I think it hurts so I usually cry. Mommy sets a timer, Beth reads me a story from Winnie the Pooh, and I cry. If I don't cry, then I hold my breath and get tense. I don't know why, it just happens that way.

I like all the stories from Winnie the Pooh, especially the one when Piglet gets rescued by Pooh because Pooh is a hero and they say he is very smart. Daddy calls me Pooh. He says I am a bear of very little brain, just like Pooh. He calls me his little Pooh bear and his koala. I also like the stories about Madeline in Paris and I like Goodnight Moon. Goodnight Moon is Mommy's favorite story as well, so we read it a lot together. Madeline is like me because she is little.

After the standing table, Beth feeds me. I don't get to taste anything, since it all goes straight into my stomach, but I like feeling full anyway. When I'm hungry, my stomach growls, and it makes me unhappy. Usually I get stiff when I'm hungry, but sometimes I cry. Mommy and Daddy always know what I need, though, so they feed me. I try not to throw up because that tastes bad and scares me. I feel like I can't breathe for a while, and sometimes I cough a lot.

I smell Mommy now. I think she's standing next to Beth. I can move my lips and, even though no sound comes out, Mommy likes it. If I move my lips sometimes I cry for no reason. If I cry, Mommy usually picks me up.

I was right. Mommy picked me up and I'm lying in her lap now. She holds my hand and brushes my hair. She's telling me all about her day and asking how I feel. I like to listen to the sound of Mommy's voice, especially when it's so close that the words brush against my ear and her lips touch my cheek. I can feel the sound on the side of my face before I even hear it. Daddy's voice is deep on my cheek and tickles. Mommy's voice is high and feels like a kiss. She is stroking my temples.

I love Mommy.

∽ ∾

I fell asleep for a long time. When I woke up, my chest was sore and I had a coughing fit. I coughed until my throat didn't feel so clogged, and then my chest felt better but I was tired again. I don't like coughing. Sometimes it makes me throw up.

A bell rang and then Mommy talked to someone while she held me on her lap. She was happy. I think she was talking to Daddy, because she talks a different way when she talks to him. She was holding me against her so that my knees were in her lap. Sometimes it's hard for me to sit that way because my whole body curls up and I can't straighten out. My tummy hurt on the *inside for a long time, and while Mommy was talking, I had to poopy, so I did. I did a big poopy, and Mommy heard it and laughed.*

She called me a stinky girl, then she kissed me.

While they were changing me, I had another coughing fit. I coughed only a few times and felt better, but my legs were cold because Mommy pulled off my pants and diaper. I cried and they put on my pants again. Mommy brought a hot water bottle and laid that across my legs as she held me. It was very warm, just like the sun, and I had trouble keeping my eyes open. I was very sleepy even though I had just woken up. It's like that for me. Sometimes the more I sleep, the sleepier I feel.

After another feeding, Beth dressed me in very warm clothes and my favorite white hat, and they carried me outside to my chair. Then Beth walked me up the road. The chair bounces a lot on the gravel. I like that. It's sort of like when they give me a leg massage. I also like the sun in my face and the wind. Wind is almost better than sun because it is a lot like constant kisses from Mommy and Daddy. I like wind best when it comes with the sun. The warm sun and the kissing wind feel good. I sighed three times on my walk.

The cars go by every now and then. I used to get scared by them, but they're not as scary anymore. They sneak up slowly, then all of the sudden there is a great roar, and then they're gone again. To me, a car seems like a big hole in the ground that you walk over and hear the noise from a waterfall when you're right over it, but then it goes away when you pass the hole.

We walked for a long time, and when I came home, Daddy was there. He picked me up out of the chair and tucked me against his chest. He has a big lap like Beth, but he holds my hand in his and puts my other hand under his arm so that they're both warm. He wraps me in a blanket and puts his one arm between my legs so that I feel like I'm being held from all directions at once. I'm comfiest in Daddy's arms, and I think I might go to sleep before he puts me down.

☙ ❧

Cheryl came sometime while I was sleeping. She is another nurse who comes all the way from Canada each day. Cheryl has a little daughter who is sick too, but she comes anyway to help Mommy and Daddy with me. I think Cheryl's daughter may be nearly as sick as I am. She's a very nice lady, but she makes me work harder than anyone else. When I do my exercises with Cheryl, I'm the most tired of all.

Tonight, Cheryl didn't make me do exercises. Instead, Mommy took me in the bath with her. I love the bath. Mommy and I get in together, and it is always very hot. At first, it stings my bottom but I like the warm feeling it gives my feet. A bath is like having sunshine hit every part of my body at once. I yawn a few times, then I start to fall asleep. Mommy thinks I fall asleep immediately, but I don't. I usually stay awake with my eyes closed for a while and think. Mommy lets me stretch out and float. My hands bob at the surface and Mommy only has to hold up my head. She says I'm so fat that I float.

You might wonder what I think about when I'm floating in the bathtub with my eyes closed. That's the best part of the story. I think about God. I try to imagine what it will be like when God holds me. You see, since my eyes don't work like everyone else's, I see different things than most kids. Mommy and Daddy think that when I tilt my head back and look at the ceiling, it has something to do with my brain not working. It doesn't though. Up high above us, I see angels dancing. Sometimes they come down close and talk to me and sometimes they are very far away, but they always seem to be dancing. And when they talk to me, they tell me that God is waiting for a little while yet to see me, and that I have a very good reason for being here. They say that when I visit God, I will sit on His lap and talk to Him for a long time, and when I fall asleep, He's going to give me to the angels to hold while I wait for Mommy and Daddy.

I like to think about that in the bathtub because I think being held by God is a lot like being held by Daddy, except better.

CHAPTER 8
Hope Rekindled

Our visit to Fred Epstein was a watershed event for a number of reasons. In part because of the character of Epstein and his colleague, Jeff Wisoff. In part because their clarity shattered so many of our assumptions. Mostly, though, because they gave us a choice, and up to that point we had had no choice.

I have never spent much time in New York City, and so have always felt slightly intimidated by the sense of boundlessness between communities. Every other city I have visited is compartmentalized, as if it is made of a number of small towns or neighborhoods that grew together yet retained their independence to some degree. Manhattan has been rebuilt on top of itself so many times that the old boundaries between neighborhoods have disappeared, and what is left is a sprawl of city, uncompartmentalized, a mosaic made up of different shades of the same color.

The lower East Side is home to Tisch Hospital, where we would meet Fred Epstein. It is typical of this boundlessness. Between 25th and 35th, the East River, and Lexington is an area filled with hospitals, the buildings of New York University, other medical facilities, countless high-rise apartments overlooking the East River, and streets and avenues dominated by four-story buildings with shops, pizza parlors, delis, art supply shops or restaurants on the ground level. It is a sprawl, incohesive. The city is all around it. Five blocks west is the Empire State Building. Seven blocks south is St. Mark's Place. Just around the corner is a neat little square and small park between Lexington and 3rd at 29th Street. But head in any direction and there is no real sense of having left the place. It is all just city. The same is true in reverse. Arriving, there is no real sense of reaching a particular destination. It is all just city.

The arrival with Elie and Liz was filled with anxiety. Tisch Hospital is a white complex, fifteen stories high and perched directly above the East River. At the top, there is a huge, blue emblem with "NYU Medical Center" written on it. The entrance is on First Avenue, overlooking five lanes of busy traffic. Patients, doctors, medical students, nurses, and visitors continually stream through the multiple sets of revolving doors. The residents all wear blue—sometimes with a white lab coat—and look young. The doctors all wear impeccably tailored suits or fine dresses with IDs clipped to the lapel. They walk the halls, trailing a dozen or so medical students or residents. The rest of us look lost.

The entrance for Epstein was actually one street down and around the corner from the main entrance to Tisch. We drove in as a family: Liz, Elie, and I riding in the back seat, Bette riding in the front and Frank driving. We brought a stroller, which we decided not to unpack when we arrived at Epstein's office building. Liz preferred to carry Elie rather than put her down. Frank pulled up to the front of a Ferrari dealership and let us out, then drove off to park the car. We waited in the atrium of the medical building, then rode up to the tenth floor together.

Epstein's office was beautifully appointed, with mahogany furniture, wallpaper with Disney characters on it, and a plush, forest green carpet. We sat down to wait. There was another young girl, perhaps fourteen years old with her mother sitting nearby. Around the corner from us, a black couple waited with a toddler in a stroller. Down from them, a father sat with a small boy. They all looked as anxious as we felt, and I realized that this was not like any other doctor's waiting room I had been in before. Other doctor's offices dealt with small concerns—ear-aches, colds, check-ups. This office dealt with life and death. Nobody in the waiting room would have ever imagined that they would be there, yet all came with the same sense of hope or fear. What would the tests show? What could this doctor do for my child? Would she or he live?

We waited a long time. Elie sat on her grandfather's lap and he made faces at her. She reached forward, and when her hand touched his face, she closed her little fist around whatever was there.

Frank laughed and Elie gurgled. The young teenager nearest us asked why we were there. Liz told her and introduced all of us. The girl, whose name was Karen, listened quietly while Liz spoke. Liz often talks to fill silences when she is nervous, and she was very nervous. Karen let the silences fall where they would. She seemed peaceful. Liz finally paused. She asked Karen why she was there. Karen explained that she had had a tumor on her cerebellum and that it had been removed in surgery. That was seven years ago. She was back for a regular check to make sure it hadn't begun growing again.

We were all silent as she spoke. Her words came like those of a grown woman and, though it was hard for me to listen because of my own concerns, we were all struck by her remarkable poise. She had had a brain tumor. They had called it "inoperable," yet Epstein had removed it. That was seven years ago and look at her now, outwardly a normal girl with strength and equanimity. She repeated a couple of times that we should hold onto our faith. "Don't give up," she said. "Whatever you do, don't give up hope."

I was heartened by Karen, and I was disturbed. Speaking with her gave me a glimpse of the future. Her tumor, its treatment, and the ever-present concern about its recurrence never left this child. There is no cure for a brain tumor. It never goes away. Even if the tumor is completely removed, it can come back. Karen had been very fortunate, she had survived her operation and the resection of part of her brain, yet she would *always* live with the knowledge that it could come back at any point—nay—that it was likely to come back. Living with a brain tumor—even after successful surgery and treatment—is like living with a time bomb in your head.

Still her courage and poise were powerful, and we all felt better for having met her. After fifteen minutes, she was called into the back room by one of the attendants. As she left, she said again. "Don't ever give up. This doctor is wonderful and God is great. Just don't give up." We thanked her and wished her luck. About three months later, we received this letter from Karen:

> *Dear Mrs. Russo,*
>
> *I'm sure you don't remember me, but I just felt I had to write to you. I met you in Dr. Epstein's office when Elizabeth went for her first appointment with him. Your family & especially Elizabeth really touched me during that one brief encounter. So much so that you all have become a part of my daily & nightly prayers. I have also followed Elizabeth's progress through Louise M____ here at Marywood.*
>
> *I'm so sorry to have heard that Elizabeth has experienced regrowth of her tumor. My heart breaks for you and your family.*
>
> *The reason, however, that I'm writing to you now is because after meeting you & your family & hearing your daughter's story, I was moved to finally sit down & write*

about my own experience & then about the many incredible people I have met along this "journey." Your daughter inspired me to sit down & write what had for seven years been my dream—I call it "Seeds of Strength." I'm sure you're not interested in reading all that I have written, but I really wanted to share with you the piece about Elizabeth.

You will all remain in my prayers in hopes that God will grant you strength and peace at this time.

Sincerely
Karen D_____

Her letter struck me. Though it came at a very hard time for us, it was the first thing to make me realize the importance of Elie's life. Here was a beautiful and poignant picture of how Elie's spiritual family was coming together, how people from different places, different lives, very different worlds, could all draw together around one, helpless little girl. Elie was pulling us together, building a family around her and—through that family—building hope. Here, in the letter from a brave child of fourteen, were the words of a true sister to Elie.

❦

We waited for forty-five minutes. I kept bothering the receptionist, mainly out of nervousness. Were we in the right place? Was Epstein still going to see us? After what seemed like an eternity, a woman opened the door to the examining rooms and called my name. I stood and she introduced herself as Tanya, Epstein's nurse practitioner.

"Dr. Epstein is still in surgery," she said. "He will probably be finishing this case up in the next thirty minutes, but then he has to go into another surgery in an hour. I'm afraid his time is very short today."

Fearing she would ask us to come back another day, my heart sank. In spite of myself, I had really begun to hope that perhaps we would hear something good here. All of the coincidences, then the words that Karen spoke, it all made me feel like Dr. Epstein might have an answer for us.

Tanya said, "Would you mind very much going across to the hospital. He has another set of offices there that are much easier for him to visit. He could see you there." She smiled.

"How do we get there?" I asked.

Again the sense of formlessness on the street, anarchy on a grid. We roll along the sidewalk, Elie in the stroller, the sounds and smells of pizza, kabob, dim sum, garbage. It is oppressive. I don't know where we're going, people are moving so fast, traffic, the light changes, we cross First Avenue. Streetlights are coming on along FDR Drive. I'm looking for a door with a marquis, the side entrance to Tisch, feeling out of control. Liz walks quietly beside me. Her parents trail close behind. It's like being in a labyrinth, looking for the doctor. The wind gusts down the avenue and takes my breath away. We cross 34th. The marquis. The entrance. A long, crowded, dirty looking hallway. Dark blue, people everywhere. People on stretchers. A security guard at the door. Blue lab coats moving all around us. Elevators around a corner. Waiting. Dark blue. Anarchy. Door closes. Fifth floor. Quiet. No sense of movement. Nobody speaks. What am I doing here? Is this really happening? It feels like hell.

We are in the room. A nurse leads us into the office behind. There is a cluttered couch, a desk, a few other chairs. A tall man in scrubs with a shock of white hair stands near the desk.

"I want my partner to take a look at your scans, if you can wait a few minutes more," he says.

Epstein leans against a huge desk and pulls at his chin. The MRI scans from Ann Arbor are on the lighted wall to our left. Epstein's arms are bare nearly to the shoulders. His skin is white and boyish, and he looks somewhat clownish in his light blue scrubs. He has a mask pulled down around his neck. His feet are covered by surgical slippers. He is well over six feet, with bright blue eyes and a lanky frame. On the wall behind him is a framed Jewish prayer. I study Epstein's face. He turns to us and smiles.

"You folks have been through a lot," he said.

We nod. His features are remarkably compassionate. Liz and I like him immediately.

"What do you see," I ask.

"I promise it will only be a few minutes more," he answers. "I'm the one who's famous," he says, "because of Reader's Digest and those things. But my specialty is really brain stem. I work on the spine and the base of the brain. Jeff Wisoff is the expert on hypothalamic tumors. He handles all the stuff in the middle of the brain. I really want him to see this. He was closing up when I left so he should be here any moment."

He steps away from the desk, lingers in front of us. "This is a terrible thing for a parent to go through," he said, looking directly at Liz. "Hang in there, kiddo. You look great." He smiled and ambled toward the door. "I'll be back with Jeff in a few moments."

Outside in the front of the office there were many people and a lot of commotion. It was all doctors and professionals, residents, nurses. No other patients waited there. I was sure they seldom saw patients in those offices. It was organized more like a retreat within the hospital. The big desk had a pizza box strewn across it. CAT scans and MRIs were everywhere. The leather couches in our office were piled with stacks of papers, the windowsills had more. It was hard to find a place to sit.

"What do you think?" I asked Liz.

"I don't know," she answered. "It seems like he knows something but doesn't want to tell us."

"I know. That seems bad," I said. "At least it can't be worse than what we know already."

We waited in silence. Elie slept on Liz's lap. Her long lashes curved upward, her lower lip hung open. She looked angelic.

After about ten minutes, Epstein returned followed by another tall man with dark hair and a handsome face. Epstein walked with an easy gait that we would come to recognize so well from a distance. Jeff Wisoff carried himself with a restrained grace, almost balletic in its formality. He was dressed in scrubs, like Epstein, but his head was bare. He introduced himself and shook hands all around.

"I wanted you to see this, Jeff," said Epstein, motioning toward the scans on the wall. "These were taken at Mott in Ann Arbor by Marasco."

"Ah, Karin," said Jeff, turning to me. "There aren't many of us in pediatric neurosurgery," he explained. "We all tend to know each other." He turned back toward the scans, his back to us now, his hands bracing himself on the table beneath the chart wall. He stood looking at one scan after another, switched a couple, compared. Without turning, he asked us, "What was the diagnosis you were given."

"P-N-E-T," I said. "A malignant tumor in the hypothalamus. They said it was inoperable."

"It's not," Wisoff said.

"It's not?" I asked, startled by his abruptness.

"No," he answered, still looking at the scans. "We've operated on this before. You have to understand, though, there are probably only 50 of these cases in the country a year. We operate on 20-30 of them. We're much more used to seeing this than they are."

I was literally dumbstruck. Of all answers, this was the one I expected least. All of our decisions now were suddenly thrown into flux. Our resolve to do nothing was based on wrong information. Or was it?

"But look," I said, "even if you can operate, it's still malignant and it's grown so fast. I don't want to end up with a child who spends her short life in the hospital going from treatment to surgery and back to treatment."

Liz chimed in. "There are four grades, right?"

Epstein nodded. "A grade-four is the most malignant."

Liz turned to Wisoff, who still had his back to us. "They told us this was a grade-four. She only has a little while. It is a grade-four, isn't it?"

Wisoff held up one finger, then turned to us.

"What do you mean," I asked him.

"It's a one. A grade-one, benign. A pilocytic astrocytoma. Don't you think, Fred?"

"That's what I thought, but I wanted to get your read," Epstein answered. "You see, they probably based their diagnosis on the fact that it was so large and she is only 8 months old. Also that she had lost mobility in her arm and face. The tumor is growing fast, much faster than a pilocytic astrocytoma should grow, but the loss of movement is from the intercranial pressure."

"The trick is," Wisoff continued, "that sometimes these benign tumors act differently in infants. They grow like a malignant tumor, but then after about two years old they stop growing or slow down."

I was shocked. None of us could speak. These words were so different from what we had expected. This morning it was hopeless. Now it didn't seem so.

"So this tumor won't kill her," I asked.

"Yes, it will. Even a benign tumor will eventually kill the patient. The fact that she has lost the use of half her body is a good sign that these problems are creating significant pressure on the brain. Looking at your scan, however, I don't think it is the tumor as much as these cysts here." He turned back to the wall and picked up a pen to point out the two black masses on each side of her brain. "These are called sub-arachnoid cysts. They are filled with fluid which generally moves through the channels of the brain keeping everything lubricated. If some of the passages become clogged, the pressure can build up and you will begin to see an increase in size, just as these show. He pointed to the lighter material next to the cysts. "This is brain tissue. As the cysts grow, they compress the brain tissue surrounding them, which cause the symptoms your daughter is showing. Eventually, the pressure would hit a vital area, like breathing, and she would die. Any operation would have to deal with these cysts as well as resect as much of the tumor as possible. That part of the operation is fairly routine, however."

We all looked at each other. This was totally unexpected. "It's a grade one?" I asked again.

"I can't be sure," Wisoff said. "The only way to be certain is to biopsy it, but that's my best guess."

"And you can operate to remove this tumor," I asked again.

"Yes," he said.

"How quickly do we have to make a decision?" Liz asked Epstein.

"It's not critical," said Epstein. "I think you should go home and talk about it. There are a lot of risks associated with surgery. You really need to think about this."

"We weren't going to do anything," Liz said. "We just wanted to make her comfortable."

"Look," Epstein said. "This is a serious tumor. It's in the worst possible place. I would not say that decision is necessarily the wrong one. Nobody would."

"But you could take out the tumor?" I asked Wisoff.

"We would take out as much as possible—I would be happy with fifty percent—then we would treat the rest with chemo. We'd try to shrink it down after resection."

"What about her eyesight," Frank asked. "Will she be blind?"

"That's a hard one to answer," Wisoff said. "The tumor surrounds the optic nerve. There is a real danger that the surgery could permanently damage her eyesight. That happened to me before. In trying to take the tumor out, I cost one boy his vision." Wisoff paused, "I have to live with that one. But it's one of the risks associated with neurosurgery."

"I could handle blindness," I said.

"We have plane tickets to take her to Lourdes," Liz said to Epstein.

Epstein answered, "Like I said, I don't think that is an unreasonable course of action. Look, her life is in God's hands. You need to think about this."

"We're supposed to leave on Monday for two weeks," Liz explained. "Should we wait until we return to schedule a surgery if that is what we choose?"

Epstein looked at Wisoff, then answered: "I wouldn't want to wait that long. This progression is fairly rapid right now. I think you need to make a decision. Perhaps you could postpone the trip to Lourdes for a while."

"How soon would you intend to operate?" I asked.

"We would admit her day after tomorrow. We could schedule surgery for Monday morning."

This was moving too fast for me. All of my decisions, my certainty, had been based on the assumption that Elie's prognosis was hopeless. If that was untrue, we had to consider a different plan. One of the options, obviously, was to stick with our original resolve. To me, however, that no longer seemed right. And yet, I had so many fears.

"My biggest fear," I tried to explain, "is that Elie ends up living a miserable life in hospitals, going through treatment after treatment and slowly wasting away. We decided we did not want that for her. If it is a choice between that and letting her go, we decided to let her go."

Epstein answered, "I think you are remarkably strong parents to have been able to make that choice. But I think there are other options here. I don't believe this is hopeless. I don't believe your daughter has to die."

"We have had other cases like this," suggested Wisoff. "A couple of families come to mind who have children that underwent this surgery two or so years ago. Both kids are doing remarkably well. Why don't I get the names and numbers of the parents and you can call to talk to them."

∽ ∾

Back on the street and for the whole ride home, we were very quiet. Nobody spoke. Epstein and Wisoff had spent another twenty minutes with us, patiently answering our questions, then answering more from Liz's father. We were out of questions, out of talk. It was as if we had believed the world was flat and found out it was round. Conclusions cannot change as quickly as assumptions. Our assumptions were so fundamentally altered.

Liz said a number of times, "Maybe this is the miracle, Kent. Maybe this is what we have been praying for." But she was as torn as I; moments later she would say with a sob, "I don't want her to die on some operating table. I just want her to die in my arms."

I, similarly, was willing to deny what we had been told. And yet I could not help but see a chance. There was a hope, however small, that my daughter could live and be normal. I was ecstatic, but I was cautious, ever so cautious, not to be swept up by unrealistic wishes into doing something I knew was wrong. My greatest fear was that we would prolong a painful existence beyond where it was meant to end, that we would cripple our child and force her to live without any real hope for the future, in a hospital, a guinea pig of the medical system.

It is funny, in retrospect, that my greatest fear largely became reality. Elie was helpless. We, by choosing to give her a chance, made her what she was, a child on a couch, unable to speak, walk, lift her arms, feed herself, or even smile. God the practical joker. He knew my greatest fear and gave it to me. And yet, by becoming real, I learned my fears were baseless. What I had feared most was not worthy of fear at all, but of admiration and love. The gift of life is never worthy of fear. Even in the worst condition we can imagine, even for our children and those we love, the gift of life is profound and worthy of reverence.

CHAPTER 9
Nine West

 I cannot remember the exact order of events after that first diagnosis in Ann Arbor, who said what, where I was, what I felt. Time entered my perception in random snippets that were dropped in a pile before entering the cubbyholes that are memory. The pile of perceptions grew, added new items, but there was no order to those perceptions—only a loose association of memory.
 That lasted until Epstein and Wisoff gave me a choice. As I sat with Liz that evening, my mind cleared and everything took shape. The world was clear, distinct. My perceptions and the thoughts surrounding them took structure. I was rational. My daughter's life rested on my decision. I had to begin filing again, understanding, asking.
 Of course, the surgery was our only choice. Elie was eight months old. We had to give her a chance at life. How could we live with ourselves if there was a reasonable—even a slim—opportunity to save her—maybe even cure her—and we ignored it? After our meeting with Wisoff and Epstein, there was no turning back. I wrestled with it, I thought a lot about it, but I knew deep in my heart that we had to try.

Liz was uncertain. She wavered back and forth. Her greatest fear was Elie dying on the table, unheld by a mother who couldn't be there at the supreme moment. The fear was almost irrational. At times, I thought Liz would rather have done nothing than take a chance at losing Elie during surgery, even if she might be cured. We talked a lot about our fears and, despite her wavering, she bowed to my certainty. I could not be shaken from the knowledge that we had to try.

It was strange how each of us in the family dwelled on our greatest fear as we contemplated this surgery. Liz's father, who has always feared losing his eyesight and has twice nearly done so, could not stop asking Wisoff and Epstein how likely total blindness was. I laughed at one point because it almost sounded as if Frank disregarded the idea of death as trivial but couldn't accept the awfulness of Elie's permanent blindness if she lived. Having a daughter who was blind for life did not give me even a moment's pause. I would have gladly accepted that.

Liz was terrified of not being with Elie when she died. If she could do nothing more for her daughter, she would at least comfort her in her last moments. Later, after the surgery when we spent long weeks in the hospital, the fear stayed with her and it was nearly impossible to convince Liz to leave the room, even to eat.

My mother was afraid, like I, that Elie's suffering would be prolonged in a vain attempt to prolong her life at all costs. My father was afraid, I think, that he would not be there for us, that the demanding obligations of his work would force him away and that he would be somewhere else when we needed help most. Both of these fears were baseless. My mother's for the same reason as mine, and my father's because his work actually brought him to New York and kept him there more than he ever had been or ever would be again. His work brought him to us rather than away for the time we were there.

But we all had fears, all—perhaps—except Liz's mother. Bette was never afraid. She was sad, to be sure. She cried over Elie, and I have seldom seen Bette cry. Yet there was no fear. She gave Elie's care over to God immediately, and she trusted in that care. Deep faith carries peace with it.

When we arrived home from the city that evening, we called the parents of the two children Wisoff had recommended. They were very understanding. One had a daughter who had just had her second birthday party. Wisoff, the mother explained, had removed about 75 percent of the tumor in surgery. Then the little girl had undergone chemo for 18 months. The last MRI scans showed the tumor had shriveled up to nothing. They considered her cured.

Liz was crying as she listened. I thought about Elie's one-year birthday party coming in September and how neither of us thought Elie would reach it. As the woman spoke, I pictured a two-year old running across the yard kicking balloons, a white dress, a party hat, her mouth crooked with the smile that I would remember as long as I live.

The woman was effusive. She explained how her daughter's development had been delayed. We all agreed that seemed like a small price to pay. "It's a miracle," the woman said a few times. "We were told it was hopeless, but it's a miracle." There was an immediate bond between us, as there is between all parents who suffer something like this. She offered to talk with us anytime, day or night, about anything at all. We thanked her and hung up the phone.

The parents of the second child had a similar story, though not quite as positive. Their son was also nearly two years old. His tumor had been 50% resected. The chemo had not been able to destroy the remaining tumor, but the tumor itself had not grown at all and seemed to be in check. Their son was pretty much normal, though also slightly delayed. We could hear him in the background.

"Would you have any reason to reconsider your choice at this point," I asked the mother.

"Never. I would do it again in a second."

Skepticism is one of my most robust attributes. I am skeptical of politics and politicians. I am skeptical of corporations. I am skeptical of media, and banks, and anyone who is prosperous but claims to have other people's interests at heart. I am skeptical of Christ and—until I met Liz—organized religion. As a journalist, my skepticism seemed boundless. When I recall these few days, however, I am surprised at how completely my skepticism deserted me. It should have been more active when we talked to the doctors and the parents. We only spoke to two sets of parents. We heard the advice of two doctors. But my skepticism was smothered by hope.

I suppose that I was less than rational. For all of the success stories, there were bound to be failures. I never asked about them. I never really thought about them. It was like buying a lottery ticket: if you concentrate on the likely outcomes, you never play. I knew there was a chance for Elie and before there had been none. It was like turning on the faucet for a man dying of thirst. I did not stop to think, I just drank.

I say my skepticism deserted me, but given the same circumstances, I would do nothing differently now. I would still opt for surgery. I remember the thought occurring to me one day as I sat and watched my five-month old son, Alex. What if I found out he had the same thing? Would I do this again? Could I go through all that we have gone through, know the possible consequences to my only other child, and make the same decision a second time?

The resounding answer has to be yes. I would have to give him a chance at life. Our hearts, our intellects, our wills are all bent toward life. We sway before its fluid substance like grass under water. Life ripples through us. It is a gift, and we treasure it in ourselves, our loved ones, particularly in our children. Of course I would choose life. What other choice could I possibly make?

My sister and her husband arrived Saturday morning. My father was scheduled to arrive Sunday morning and stay with us Sunday afternoon until we had to go in, then he would drive with us or take a train to the city and his hotel. We had called to arrange for Elie's admittance to the hospital. Liz spoke to Jeff Wisoff, who said that the nurse practitioner would take care of all the details.

Tanya returned our call an hour later. We were to register at Tisch Hospital the following afternoon between 4 and 5 pm. Surgery was scheduled for Monday at 7 am. I thanked her and hung up.

There was still a lot of chatter around the table that night, still smiles and laughter. But the laughter was strained. The smiles sometimes seemed forced. My sister cried when she held Elie. The sound made Liz cry. The rest of the people at the table tried hard to keep the meal from turning mournful. Someone picked up the conversation and we carried on. It was so hard to hold Elie without thinking how short the time might be until we could hold her no more.

Elie had gotten noticeably worse. Half of her mouth was now completely paralyzed and sagged at the corner. She still smiled a wobbly smile, but her hands didn't work well. Liz had a bonnet tied around her head, and it made her look small and frail, already much different than the child from just three days ago. She was a happy child but she seemed, pathetically, to be losing her struggle. We talked about calling Tanya back to let her know how poorly Elie was doing. We decided to wait until morning.

The day before I arrived in New York and before our meeting with Epstein and Wisoff, Liz was filming a video of the family taking turns playing with Elie. She stood in the doorway of the kitchen and filmed into a dark room that was lit only by the hanging lamp above the dinner table. Frank sat at his end, reading mail. A couple of other siblings lounged back in their chairs, the table mostly cleared before them. Bette washed dishes. It seemed so normal. A friend of the family, Ilucion, was holding Elie beneath the arms so that she could stand on the table. Elie bounced on the table as if she were in her Jolly Jumper, and then, without warning, she stopped and said loudly and repeatedly, "Da-da" "Da-da.... Da-da-da-da-da-da-da.... Da-da-da-da-da-da-da." Liz zoomed in to a close up of Elie's face.

Elie spoke for thirty to forty seconds. It was the only time she ever spoke that we know of, and Liz happened to catch it on video. I watched it the evening I arrived, laughing through the tears. I've watched it many times since. "I'm here," I say to the image on the screen. "I'm listening to you, little darling." My daughter's voice, now silent, calling to me from the past. "I hear you."

Elie slept in bed with us, between us. Things had not really changed much in that sense. She was still fussy, she still wanted to nurse often, she still woke early. We talked late that night, facing each other with Elie's bald head between us, fast asleep. I no longer remember what we talked about. I am sure it was Elie, how much we loved her, how so many people were praying for her, how things had changed so fast, how frightened we were about Monday, how different Elie was now. Thinking about where my life was taking me, I drifted into an uneasy sleep.

I woke at seven and took a car to pick up my father at LaGuardia. The Russos were just rising and getting ready for church. My sister and her husband were sitting at the table, drinking orange juice. Twenty-four hours and my daughter's head would be opened up on an operating table. Julie and Steve tried to seem cheerful.

"Do you want us to come with you?" Julie asked.

"Nah," I said. "No reason to. You might as well stay here and enjoy the sunny morning."

"I think we'll go to church with the Russos," Julie said. "For Elie." I was not surprised, though my sister had never attended church. It almost seemed natural with Elie. She drew us to her and toward God. Julie smiled sheepishly. "It can't hurt," she said.

Liz stepped into the kitchen carrying Elie, who was awake and dressed for church. She was trying to smile but she had trouble moving. She couldn't lift her arm at all. I looked at her for a bit. I talked to her and kissed her cheek. She made a soft cooing sound. "She seems so weak," I said.

"I'm worried that she's gotten worse," Liz said. "Maybe we should call Epstein."

"I don't think they're going to do anything today unless it's really an emergency."

"Maybe this is an emergency," Liz said.

I picked up the keys to the car. "Call the number he gave us. He said 'anytime, day or night.' The answering service will reach him or Tanya. Talk to them about her. I'll be back in an hour."

My father Walter was waiting on the curb at LaGuardia when I arrived. He hugged me and kissed my cheek. "Taxi's here," I said.

When we arrived back at the Russo home, Liz was standing in the driveway with Elie. The back of the wagon was open with bags packed inside. Frank was adjusting the child seat and strapping it in.

"They want us to go in now," she said. She kissed my father. The worry showed in her face. Elie was beautiful in blue. My father set his bags down. "Well, I had better get a cab to the train station and catch a train in," he said. "You have a full car here." Walter did not want to be in the way, but he knew this was hard on me. I tried not to show my heavy heart. Things were moving so fast, and we wouldn't even be able to have one last comfortable breakfast in the sunshine before we went.

We stood there for a moment. Liz looked at me. I think she must have read my mind. "Do you want to hold Elie," Liz asked Walter.

"Come inside and have a quick bite to eat. You can hold Elie through breakfast."

◈ ◈

The second drive into Tisch was different than the first. I paid no attention to the surroundings until we arrived. We stared down at Elie, talked to her, held her hand. Liz nursed her as best she could, and Elie gurgled. She was clothed in a baby blue dress with a frilled collar and sun hat. Her mouth sagged at us but she tried to smile a lot.

Once inside, we made our way through registration. I signed forms, discussed meal plans, signed more forms, accepted a folder with information I would never read, heard about my rights as a patient, paid no attention, and then followed directions to the elevators that would take us to the ninth floor and our room in the West Wing. I became the troop leader and the guide. It helped me to get through this. At least if I was leading, I was doing something for someone. Liz needed to ignore the details. I could tell she had to harness all of her strength to keep focused on Elie. I myself needed some way to do something—anything—that would help Liz or Elie. For me, doing nothing—feeling helpless—was the hardest part.

The Tisch building opens into an inner courtyard with cement steps, some shrubs, a few trees and a lawn. It is deep in the center of the building, so mid-summer sun might only reach the lawn for a few hours a day, but it is pleasant. The main floor hallway surrounds the courtyard. It is decorated with sculptures and glass walls, boards with artwork on them and plaques listing founding donors. The doors leading away into side halls and offices are amber wood and give the hallway a rich feeling. Around a few corners and toward the back of the building are the triple elevators, framed by green and black marble. People idle here because the elevators oppose the doors opening into the courtyard. In between, there is an open waiting area with art-deco armchairs and tables filled with magazines. Residents and nurses lounge outside or in the armchairs, eat lunch, drink coffee. Groups of hospital workers smoke and chat together.

Our arrival means nothing to any of these people. We will come to know some of the nurses, a few residents, the same number of doctors. But we are just one of a long line of people with problems who come to Tisch for help. I will realize this later, but don't at this point. I am still filled with the disbelief that this has happened to us. To my family, Elie's case is unique. Our child with a brain tumor has stopped our world and spun it the opposite direction. For some irrational reason, I assume it has done so for everyone else. Only later, I realize that the tumor itself is nothing special to any of these people. Tumors enter and leave their lives daily. If we are to touch their hearts—and to my great surprise when I look back, I think we did—it is because of something besides the brain tumor. It is because of our love and the love we share with Elie. That love is something special in a world of white walls and people who have seen more suffering and heartache than any person should.

∽ ∾

Floor Nine. We step out of the elevator into the hallway that would be our home for six weeks or more. We did not know that at the time either. We expected to be there a week or maybe two, as Wisoff had suggested.

The halls are painted pink and the lights are fairly dim. The rooms are yellow or cream colored. We pass a series of doors as we make our way toward our own. Each room has one or two patients, all children. Inside many, often clustered together or sprawling on chairs, are the families of the child. Curtains obscure most of the children, but the families sit at the ends of the beds. They look up when we pass. We manage a weak smile. Some smile back.

Other parents walk the hall with their children in strollers. A couple with a small boy passes us. Another boy wearing a helmet wanders by, towing a pole with an IV pump and med bag. His mother walks behind him, watching carefully. Nurses zip from room to room, working fast and efficiently. One nurse looks at my papers and points us in the direction we were going. In an alcove to the right are a number of wheelchairs. On the wall there are diagrams of the brain, notice boards, colored posters done by children in a school and sent to the kids in the hospital. The posters have names and ages of the artists scrawled on them in crayon.

Nine West. The pediatric, neuro-oncology wing. It is a sobering walk to our room. And all that waiting. People sitting on chairs beside small, frail bodies, helpless to do anything. I want to go home. This is exactly what I am most afraid of. Hopelessness and slow withering. I steady myself. I will give my daughter a chance. Though I am afraid of this for myself, I will give her a chance at life.

There is another couple with a young girl in the room when we arrive. Liz speaks to them for quite a while, especially with the mother. I cradle Elie. Kiss her face. Hold her hand. She is sleeping. She looks like an angel. The other couple is young. They have Slavic accents and introduce themselves. I nod but forget their names immediately. He is short and neatly dressed with a salt and pepper beard, very carefully trimmed. The woman is pretty but her hair is messed and her clothes very wrinkled. It is easy to see she has been through a lot. The child, which, she explains, they adopted from Yugoslavia, has had severe stomach problems and cannot gain weight. He vomits repeatedly after every feeding. The doctors are concerned the problem may be tumor related. Liz speaks a lot with them about our mutual concerns.

Our room looks out toward Brooklyn, across the East River and Robbins Island. To the left is the Citgo sign and the Queensborough

Bridge. To the right are the piers and docks of Brooklyn and, above those, Brooklyn Heights' brick apartments and the stacks of a power plant. We pile our stuff in the corner, bags of clothes, a couple of books, more bags of food. Bette begins to arrange things and pack Elie's clothes into the two drawers allotted to us. I speak with the nurse, sign more papers, watch while they place the ID tag around Elie's wrist, thank the nurse, sit down. And then we wait.

Being in a hospital is mostly waiting. Waiting for the doctor. Waiting for medicines. Waiting for your operation. Waiting while your body recovers. It is a chore because medicine, while it can relieve pain and ensure recovery, cannot speed the natural healing powers of time and the human organism. You simply have to wait. The waiting room is stark, sterile. A TV hangs from the ceiling but that does not make time pass faster, it only fills it with a knobby substance that doesn't really fit well in the empty vessel formed by time. And the doctor's care is all about waiting. After the few moments or few hours of intervention, during which you are unconscious so you are not actually waiting, the doctors simply monitor to make sure that nothing slows the process of healing. They visit you once or twice a day. Otherwise they wait and you wait with them, almost aching for something besides empty time.

An hour later, a resident arrives to greet us. He wears a blue hospital outfit and a white lab coat. He introduces himself as a neurosurgery resident and says he has come to explain the process leading up to surgery. Tony is friendly and smiles a lot. I speak with him as cheerfully as I can, instinctively wanting to befriend any doctor who might have some responsibility for my little girl on the operating table. He tells us that we are not to feed her after midnight. He asks if we have any other questions.

"Is Wisoff a good surgeon?" I ask.

"He and Epstein are the best," Tony says without hesitating. "I had a choice of a dozen residency programs, the best hospitals and a lot of them nicer than New York. I came here, though, because of Epstein and Wisoff. You're in good hands."

After Tony leaves, quiet descends on our room. The other child is tiny and has fallen asleep. Her parents have stepped out for a bite to eat. Liz holds a set of Rosary beads. Bette sits in the chair and reads a prayer book. I hold Elie. The late-afternoon sun is slowly sinking, lighting up the buildings across the river as it goes. It is strange, sitting in a hospital room, far above the city streets, looking toward the East and the shadows lengthening across the water, the skyline stretching horizontally toward Brooklyn, lights coming on and the traffic moving more slowly over the Queensborough Bridge. Two weeks ago we were home on the lake, preparing for spring. I was turning my garden over and raking out the beds. The ice had gone out a month before. The water had turned from slate gray to a deep blue. Crocuses and daffodils were poking up through the mulch I had carefully laid across the beds in the front. It was a world away from our room in Nine West. We had been taken out of time, out of the progression of seasons, away from everything that anchored life in a definable, understandable process. I hold my daughter in a room where the temperature never varies by more than a few degrees, where the windows cannot open to let in a fresh breeze or the smells of the city, where passing time is marked by the change in the nursing shifts rather than anything natural. In twelve hours, Elie will lie on the operating table. I might not see her again. Nine West is unnerving.

Liz takes Elie from me and they fall asleep for a short while in Elie's crib. Liz slept worse than I the night before and was exhausted. Her right hand is tucked under the corner of her pillow, her left arm is wrapped around Elie. She has a couple of small receiving blankets pulled over their backs and across her legs. She looks worn. Elie's mouth droops open.

Bette sets down her book and stands. I watch her but am too tired to say anything. "I'm going to pick up some food for us," she says. "How about pizza?"

"Fine," I answer. I should probably offer to go for her, but I am too tired. I am too tired even to get up. I cannot think about tomorrow now.

The only person who is really comfortable and at ease is Elie. She is too young to know what she faces. All she knows is the warmth of lying by her mother's side, being held, talked to, rocked, kissed. It is an ironic blessing that the child facing mortal danger knows nothing of that danger. How much more difficult this would be if, in addition to our own fears, we had to respond to hers.

I drift into an uneasy sleep, sitting upright in a hospital chair at the foot of Elie's crib. Now I am part of the group I saw when we first came in, the weary family, slumped in chairs around the bed, visible to those passing in the hallway. Now I am a parent of one of the children whose life hangs in the balance. And I am waiting at the foot of the bed to see how it turns out. I am one of them, powerless to change the course of events that has taken control of my daughter's life. And tomorrow they will cut away a piece of her skull and probe down into her brain.

And I think as I fall asleep: thank God this will only be for a week or two.

*   *

Around 11 pm Elie grows very hungry. Liz is upset because the one means of solace for Elie has always been breast feeding, and she is not allowed to do that. The doctors want Elie's stomach empty for surgery. Liz and I take turns strolling Elie around the halls, her cries sharp and loud. It is very hard on Liz. All she wants to do is lift Elie to her breast and give her peace. Elie twists her head in Liz's arms and mouths her sweater looking for a breast.

In the middle of the night, Liz is strolling past a door on the opposite hallway. There is a light on and Liz looks into the room. A young woman who looks about 25, no older than Liz or I, sits at the foot of the bed. She smiles at Liz and says something about how frantic Elie's cries sound. Liz answers and the woman comes out into the hallway. They talk for a while. The woman, named Didi, has been on Nine West for six weeks. Her son, Bobby, is less than a year. He has a malignant brain tumor in the advanced stages, she explains to Liz. They have been through surgery twice. Bobby had pneumonia following the first. They are on their third chemo regime. The last time they had an MRI, it showed the tumor had metastisized in other parts of his body, down his spinal cord, in his lung.

"It must have been very hard knowing you would be coming in here for so long," Liz said.

Didi laughed ruefully. "We thought we were coming in for a week the first time," she said. "It has just gotten worse so that even when we do leave, we know we'll be back in a few days or a week."

Liz is a wonderful person and full of joy. I am sure as she talked to Didi, she showed none of her growing apprehension at what she heard. She probably touched his small head, said nice things to him, told Didi what a great mother she was and how well she obviously cared for him. At the end of their conversation, I can imagine Didi felt refreshed and even cheerful. Liz has that effect on people.

But when she returned to me, she was crying. I was dozing in one of the fold-down hospital chairs. She shook me with her hand and said she had to talk to me. It was three in the morning. There were tears in her eyes as she told me she didn't think she could go through with the operation. By this point, I had resolved myself and was simply waiting, wishing it were over already and that the results were good. For me, there was no choice anymore, and so we had to wait for resolution and hope for the best. Liz, on the other hand, was shaken at the very foundation of our decision to treat Elie. She told me all about Bobby, and I listened to her. How withered he looked. How unhappy he seemed. One week stretching into 6... 8... 14. "I don't want to go through with this," she ended. "I don't want to do that to my baby."

"His is a totally different case," I said. "His is malignant. Ours might not be malignant." I went on and on, listing our reasons. I was rational. My arguments were logical. Bobby's parents had no real hope anymore. I agreed with her that I would never let Elie get to that point. We would let her go before that. They were good arguments and I knew they were right, at least at an intellectual level.

But Liz's response was not intellectual. It was visceral, and it came from the mix of fear, anxiety, and the hopelessness that our position forced on her. We were speaking two different languages, yet I knew how she felt. At the very fundament, we shared a similar fear—the same fear every parent has—of putting one's child through suffering for no purpose. From our perspective, we could not see any purpose to her suffering. That understanding only comes later, long after.

I do not intend to judge the actions of Bobby's parents by what I have said here. Each parent makes his or her own decision, and each decision is the right one as long as it is made out of love for the child. I think Bobby's mother and father nurtured some small sliver of hope that they could save him. They were treating him in a great hospital. They had the best doctors. Bobby's father said to me one night as I sat with them: "He's doing worse each week, but we have to try anyway. We can't do nothing." He was right, at least for them. For us, however, it was not right, and all we could think was that we might be faced with that same horrible situation.

Elie did not quiet down much that night. She was frantic for Liz's breast and could smell the milk that leaked out on Liz's shirt. Her tortured cries were breaking Liz's heart. I took Elie to the other wing for a while and strolled the hallways for an hour or so. She quieted a bit, but would only remain so for a few moments, then she would wake again and start crying. I passed our room at one point and Liz, who was lying in the crib and had only had a few hours sleep in the past two days, jumped up and took her from me.

"I don't care what they say," Liz said. "I may not have her tomorrow. I'm going to let her have what she needs tonight."

"You shouldn't," I tried to argue. "Only give her a little."

Liz crawled back into the crib with Elie, who suckled for no more than a couple of minutes before falling fast asleep, wrapped in her mother's arms. I watched them for a little while. I was proud of Liz. Her love for her only child could be fearsome.

And, as I look back, I am happy. That night, lying together, Liz cradled Elie's head against her breast, warmed her small body, wrapped her in blankets and mother's comfort. It was a poignant moment, shaded in the dim light of the hospital room at 4 am. The curtain was pulled up around the crib. The sounds of the city were lost. Everything was quiet except the soft chatter from the nurse's station down the hall. Mother and daughter had one last moment together the way they had been since Elie's birth. It was the last time Elie would ever nurse.

Middle Interlude

Once a month or so my work takes me on a long trip, usually by car. I do not mind driving, particularly if I can travel the smaller roads by day, but I have a bad habit of falling asleep at the wheel. I stop for coffee every couple of hours and play the radio, tuned to whatever talk radio station I can pick up.

One week, I was making the journey back from Madison, Wisconsin. I left around 4 pm with snow showers threatening and two good hours of light left. The drive from Madison to Green Bay was not bad, and I made it without stopping, listening the whole time to NPR news. From Green Bay, I drove to Marinette, and from there I crossed into Michigan and followed Route 35 along the lake and the long stretches of sand beaches and small cottages toward US 2, where I would begin the backstretch across Michigan's Upper Peninsula toward home. As I drove Route 35, the snow picked up and the radio stations grew increasingly infrequent.

About halfway to Escanaba, the snow hit hard. Lake effect squalls were dropping big flakes in sudden bursts. It was dark, and my headlights reflected the streaks of snow in a hypnotic rhythm that made it very hard to keep my eyes open. If it had been steady, I would have stopped for the night in Escanaba, but it let up occasionally and gave me a chance to rest and reach for the tuning button to find the next talk station. Each seemed fainter than the last, leaving me with the pleasant feeling I always have returning to the U.P. that I am moving away from civilization. Now and then I hit on a station that seemed strong, but after ten minutes, like the snow squalls, it would disappear again.

I listened to a financial show where the host gave advice on everything from home mortgages to starting a business. It was broadcast from Chicago, and it faded quickly. I changed the channel and found the same show on a different station, running about fifteen minutes behind the first. I got to listen to the same somnolent voice a second time.

I switched to some music when that disappeared, but the music soon made me sleepy so I hit the tuner button again, stepping up the AM dial in single increments. I could not tune anything in very well and feared I had lost the radio for the night, when suddenly I picked up a strong signal from a Chicago station. I was driving the lakeshore and must have entered an area where the signal had a clear path across the ice. It was my financial show just finishing up, and the signal was clear and loud. The host signed off, a theme jingled pleasantly, and the commercials started.

I was about fifteen minutes from Escanaba and it was dark. The snow had stopped but the roads were slick. A strong radio station was a blessing. I slipped my shoes off and turned up the heat a bit. As long as I had a good talk show, I could afford to be a little warmer. I smiled as I thought of my children. My second child, Alex, was over six months old then and very active. I knew he was probably nursing at that moment and ready to fall asleep. I thought about Elie, as I always do when I drive. She would be in the nurse's arms, her cheeks flushed, her eyes just barely open, quiet on the couch and nearly asleep as well. At nine o'clock, she gets her night medicines: a crushed steroid tablet and two syringes of oral anti-seizure drugs. They usually put her to sleep, at least for a while.

Liz would be dressed in long-johns, her legs drawn up on the Queen Anne chair beside the fire, Alex in her arms. She would have shaken her hair out to its full length, turned the lights down for the baby. She might be reading. I longed to return. It is a good thing to be a father, and I feel very lucky to have the family I have. It is funny to me to think that I am grateful for a child with a brain tumor. Yet I am, and not only because the other option is that I could have lost her already. I am grateful because of the love she has brought into our house. That small, misshapen body and beautiful face are an awesome blessing. Of course I am grateful for her.

The announcement for the new show aired, the host's voice boomed out. It was a political radio program with a host who sounded like the human equivalent of a howitzer. I had never heard of him, but in his opening comments he took special care to insult and ridicule enough other perspectives that he would generate phone calls. From this early introduction, I could tell he was the liberal equivalent of Rush Limbaugh. In spite of how much I disliked the shouting matches that these types of show inevitably degenerate into, it was just the sort of show that would keep me awake.

He started by phoning a representative of one of the pro-life groups, called Operation Rescue. They talked for a while and remained fairly civil. The fellow from Operation Rescue was a Texan and sounded like he was speaking from a payphone on the main street in Dallas. They talked about a new plan Operation Rescue had for picketing outside schools to demonstrate to kids that crime, abortion, and violence were not acceptable.

Somewhere in this conversation they began to argue. The Texan was nervous and had the disadvantage of having to talk very loud anyway because the phone line was poor and the host could easily talk over him. They started shouting about God and whether God exists.

The Texan repeated again and again, "Just tell me. Are you an atheist?" And the host shouted back, "My listeners know what I am. You prove to me that God exists, you lunatic."

"Are you an atheist?"

"Are you a right-wing lunatic?"

"Just tell me. Are you an atheist?"

"Would you bomb an abortion clinic?"

I was nearly ready to turn the radio off and take my chances with sleepiness. I don't mind a good argument, but this name-calling is like listening to third-graders on the playground, just irritating. The host, I think, sensed that a lot of his listeners were ready to switch off so he stopped. Then he asked the Texan, in a much quieter tone, "Who is your God? Describe him to me."

The Texan was still full of voltage, and though he tried to calm his answer, he sounded a bit haywire. He said something like, "My God is the God of love, the prince of peace. He is the way, the truth, and the light...." And off he went, quoting scripture, which only seemed to irritate the host again. The host kept trying to break in on the Texan's speech, but the Texan never let up.

Finally, a little exasperated, the host shouted into the microphone. "Listen, shut up for just one minute and answer me this question: 'If God is the God of love, then why did he create brain tumors?'"

Why did God create brain tumors?

It hit me like a punch. What a question, I thought, posed, as it was by a radio talk show host trying to win an argument. It was nothing but a cheap trick. It was meant to stump someone who believed in God, to make him sound zealous or stupid, and it was asked by a person who probably had no experience with brain tumors other than having read about one sad story or another in the Chicago Tribune. It was a gimmick, chosen because brain tumors are such frightening things, especially to those who never experience them. A question as enigmatic and ultimately purposeless as, "If God is all good, why did he create evil?" Perhaps for other people this trick worked. For me it fell completely flat.

The Texan tried to answer. He said something about how God didn't create brain tumors. Rather, they were a result of sin and suffering brought about because Eve ate of the forbidden tree of knowledge. He knew nothing about brain tumors either, and they both soon stumbled back into name calling.

"Why did He create brain tumors?"

"You're an atheist, aren't you?"

"Why did He create brain tumors?"

"You're an atheist, aren't you?"

"Why did He create brain tumors?"

I suddenly felt sorry for them both. To them, God was a tool. They used God and argued about Him in a small-minded effort to prove a point. It was empty arguing, and I wondered if either of them really knew what they were saying, or if the purpose to them was one-upmanship for the sake of seeming smarter to themselves. They were like two men trying to gather an army behind them that was bound to march off in the wrong direction. To me, their lives seemed suddenly empty. God was a long way from their beliefs. These radio interlocutors were the modern Pharisees.

But the question reminded me of one of the most moving passages in the gospels. It comes when Jesus cures the blind beggar on the steps of the temple. Before he does so, the disciples ask:

> *"Rabbi, who sinned, this man or his parents, that he was born blind?" Jesus answered, "Neither hath this man sinned nor his parents, but that the works of God should be revealed in him... and he spat on the ground and healed the man with his spit and mud."*

I wanted to call the radio show because I did know what they were talking about. I knew about brain tumors and living with them. This is what I wanted to tell them:

"I have a little girl who is three and a half years old. She is a lovely child, and she has a brain tumor. I have this to say as one who lives intimately with a brain tumor. Don't be afraid. It isn't evil. It brings pain and sorrow, but that doesn't make life bad. In fact, in many ways it is beautiful.

"I know you can't understand what I'm saying. But the brain tumor itself is neither good nor bad, it is merely a form of suffering. And suffering itself is neither good nor evil. Rather, good and evil come from how we live with our suffering.

"God did not create brain tumors as an evil to inflict upon us; the tumor in itself is not good or bad. He did and does, however, create beautiful little girls. Brain tumors may be a way for God to touch us through those little girls. Do you want me to tell you more about a beautiful little girl?..."

※ ※

> *So the Lord said to Satan, "All right, he is in your power, but you are not to kill him." Then Satan left the Lord's presence and made sores break out all over Job's body. Job went and sat by the garbage dump and took a piece of broken pottery to scrape his sores. His wife said to him, "You are still as faithful as ever, aren't you? Why don't you curse God and die?"*
>
> *Job answered, "You are talking nonsense! When God sends us something good, we welcome it. How can we complain when he sends us trouble?" Even in all this suffering Job said nothing against God.*

The truth is that God brings suffering into our lives because suffering brings us closer to Him. This is the beauty hidden in a brain tumor. It is a key that unlocks the box filled with love, hope, generosity, beauty, care, gentleness. A box that is the opposite of Pandora's Box, because beneath all these we find our mortality.

Though it is an ungainly statement, a quote I read recently serves my point. Gordon Sherman was quoted by Paul Hawken as saying,

> "There is a teasing irony: we spend our lives evading our own redemption. And this is naturally so because something in us knows that to be fully human we must experience pain and loss. Therefore, we are at ceaseless effort to elude this high cost, whatever the price, until at last it overtakes us. And then in spite of ourselves we do realize our humanity. We are put in worthier possession of our souls. Then we look back and know that even our grief contained our blessing."

Question: Why did God create brain tumors?
Answer: Because He loves us.

> God said:
> What holds up the pillars that support the earth? Who laid the cornerstone of the world? In the dawn of that day the stars sang together, and the heavenly beings shouted for joy.
>
> Who closed the gates to hold back the sea when it burst from the womb of the earth? It was I who covered the sea with clouds and wrapped it in darkness. I marked

a boundary for the sea and kept it behind bolted gates. I told it, "So far and no farther! Here your powerful waves must stop."

Job, have you ever in all your life commanded a day to dawn?

The real question is not "Why did God create brain tumors?"

It is: "Where does the strength come from to live with our suffering."

∽ ∾

Liz has a cousin who died last year of a drug overdose. He was a happy-go-lucky man with a warm heart, a predilection for dishonesty, and a terrible set of addictions. Everyone in the family loved him, though nobody knew how to help him. The drug overdose was a surprise. Apparently he died while his 'friends' were partying around him. The autopsy showed that they only brought him to the hospital six hours after he died, and then they left him there and drove away.

His death has been a terrible burden for his mother, Liz's aunt. She sank into a depression, and eighteen months later that had only gotten worse. I believe she felt some sense of obligation or failure for having let him reach the point where he could die from his addictions. She did not immediately find the strength to understand or move beyond her grief and self-recrimination. In time she did, but it did not come easy. She had a life with many disappointments and, though she has two other wonderful sons, and five grandchildren, it is the perceived failure with her lost son that hurts.

But the lesson that Elie has taught me is that each life follows its own course, designed and directed by God. His message to Job was that we cannot hope to understand the complexity of the life that surrounds us. What appears bad to us now, when looked at from some distant space or time may actually be good. Suffering is something we will all experience. It is woven into our lives to give us the opportunity to gain strength and to choose beatitude. If our choice is right, it brings us closer to God.

Why did God give my daughter a brain tumor? I do not know. I cannot hope to know. But He did, and it has brought a blessedness to our home and our lives that never would have entered there otherwise.

The funeral mass for Liz's cousin was led by Father Delaney, a very old friend of the Russo's and a *de facto* member of the family. He knew all the kids and all the cousins from boyhood, had dinner with them every Tuesday, baptized and confirmed many of them, married a few, baptized the grandchildren, including Elie. He addressed the question that was on the minds of the family. "Where was Liz's cousin now?" He had done so many bad things, had given up the church, spent time in jail, stolen, lied. Yet he was, at the core, a generous, caring person. Nothing he ever did was malicious, but much of it was wrong. Where was he now?

Father Delaney answered this way:

> *"If we were sitting in judgment, is there any question that any one sitting among us today would forgive him his many faults, forgive his trespasses, and accept him into Heaven? Would any of us, having known him, consign him to eternal damnation?"*

He paused.

> *"How much greater is God's mercy than our own. Can there be any doubt that God as a father would be less merciful to Patrick than us?"*

Some time later God tested Abraham; He called to him, "Abraham!" And Abraham answered, "Yes, here I am!"

"Take your son," God said, "your only son, Isaac, whom you love so much, and go to the land of Moriah. There on a mountain that I will show you, offer him as a sacrifice to me."

Early the next morning Abraham cut some wood for the sacrifice, loaded his donkey, and took Isaac and two servants with him. They started out for the place that God had told him about. On the third day Abraham saw the place in the distance. Then he said to his servants, "Stay here with the donkey. The boy and I will go over there and worship, and then we will come back to you."

Abraham made Isaac carry the wood for the sacrifice, and he himself carried a knife and live coals for starting the fire. As they walked along together, Isaac spoke up, "Father!"

He answered, "Yes, my son?"

Isaac asked, "I see that you have the coals and the wood, but where is the lamb for the sacrifice?"

Abraham answered, "God himself will provide one." And the two of them walked on together.

When they came to the place which God had told him about, Abraham built an altar and arranged wood on it. He tied up his son and placed him on the altar, on top of the wood. Then he picked up the knife to kill him. But the angel of the Lord called to him from heaven, "Abraham, Abraham!"

"Don't hurt the boy or do anything to him," he said. "Now I know you have obedient reverence for God, because you have not kept back your only son from me."

At 9:32 am on May 16, 1994, Liz and I rode with our only daughter, Elizabeth Nyanga Gilges, down an elevator to the fifth floor, and carried her from there down a long corridor to a set of red, swinging doors beyond which doctors, nurses, and orderlies, all dressed in green scrubs, moved quickly and efficiently through the halls and into the operating rooms. We were stopped at the door by two surgical nurses, also dressed in scrubs, who raised their masks to explain that they would take our daughter from here. Liz cried and kissed Elie's face as lovingly as I have ever seen a mother do. I held my daughter to my chest, kissed her neck and cheek and then handed her to the nurse. "You will take good care of her," I said. They assured us they would, kissed Elie on the cheek and, as Liz stood, sobbing and bereft, carried her away from us, cradled in their own arms. We watched Elie turn the corner, her little naked body with only a diaper and an IV attached to her arm. We both cried as I led my small, heartbroken wife back to the elevator and to the room on Nine West where we would spend an eternity waiting for the results of surgery.

Part II

CHAPTER 10
Waiting

Last week, I drove with a friend to tend our bee hives for the first time since installing them this spring. We had a long, cold aftermath to winter that lingered through the end of May. Before the first of June, we never had temperatures above 55, and then—all of a sudden—it was 75 degrees. The flowers burst out, the leaves opened, there was whirring everywhere and Steve and I drove out to the bees.

We keep the eleven hives in a field near a strawberry farm. It is one of the old Polish farms that still cuts hay with a team of horses and that barely survives. The fellow next door is 70 and grows alfalfa. Across the road is a family in a wooden shack with a big plowed garden out front. There are almost no young families here anymore. The strawberry plants are compact and in neat rows, but growing them is more a hobby for the owner than a real business. He gives his strawberries away to anyone he knows, and that is everyone except the odd tourist who finds his way back there. The intermittent houses around him are set in wide expanses of field that stretch far into the distance, bounded everywhere by a distant ring of forest, yet seemingly boundless and in contact with the sky.

I was in a hurry. Liz was home with the kids. I had work to take care of, remodeling in the house, a dozen things to do. Steve was never in a hurry. Even though he ran a very large and demanding business, he drove 45 mph everywhere and always took time to stop and talk. He even talked slow. Sometimes I found it wonderful, but other times my internal clock was ticking and I wanted to get moving.

We got dressed in the barn where we kept our equipment. We loaded up the back of the truck. Steve walked out into the strawberry patch to see how the berries were coming, and I looked around exasperatedly, hoping to hurry him along with my sense of urgency. "You in a hurry?" he asked me.

"No," I said, "just things to do like always."

I actually felt bad rushing him since I knew it was harder for him to get away from his business than for me. Still, I was hoping to get back to work in the afternoon. He ambled over to the truck, asked if we had everything, and then we climbed in and drove slowly out to the bees.

Our hives were on top of a small hill, just above the strawberry patch. They were set back against a wood and surrounded by electrified barbed wire to protect them from bears. The view looked down over the alfalfa, green beneath a blue sky. The trees were vivid, the smell of spring was everywhere. Steve lit the smoker and we began opening the hives, checking them for disease, looking for the queen, assessing the need for spring feeding.

Beekeeping is a wonderfully methodical pastime. It soothes one to open up a small world so perfectly ordered, so intricately designed to benefit the species and the world around it. I hurried Steve through the first couple of hives, but when we paused in the middle to get a breath and pull off our headnets, I leaned against the tailgate, looked up at the sky, and suddenly asked myself why I was hurrying through this. I was lucky to be doing one of my favorite things in life, out in the country, in a beautiful pasture surrounded by forests and fields that stretched on for miles, smelling spring air, warm under the sun, and listening to the steady hum of thousands of bees buzzing back and forth above me as they foraged. Why was I hurrying to finish something that I loved?

Sometimes, we need to forget what we suppose are our obligations and enjoy the lives God has given us. The bees for me were an obligation, one of many. I had to tend them, but it was something I loved doing. So is it with my children. They are hard at times. Parenting is an obligation and a responsibility beyond what I expected, but it brings me tremendous joy. The worry that we develop as parents may come from a misplaced sense that we should control the environment that surrounds our kids—and in some ways, we should. But in some ways, we never can. Good living is finding reassurance in surrender. My will can only carry us so far; God's will is the way.

<hr />

We spent much of that afternoon in the courtyard, all together, speaking little. Liz's family said the Rosary for Elie. I stood at the edge and joined them sometimes, though it was hard to concentrate on anything. I decided as a small sacrifice for Elie that I would stand throughout the six-hour operation. Now it seems ridiculous. Then, I wanted to take away her pain. I wanted to suffer in her place, in any way possible.

The sun was high above when we first entered the courtyard, and the crabapple blossoms were bright and lovely. The place was a lot like the courtyard in Michigan, yet more cloistered. The sun lit only the central patch of grass. Shadows clung around the edges. By the time the grass was all in the shadow of the building and the afternoon had mostly passed, my legs were tired and I felt terribly weary. I stood beside Liz, listened to them recounting the sorrowful mysteries, and thought about my little girl, lying on a table with her head opened up.

It is comforting in some ways to be in a position where one knows that there is nothing more one can do, except, of course, pray. There is a sort of peace, albeit an anxious peace, in being truly helpless.

And prayer. Did I pray, hoping that it would help? I prayed, but did I really hope it would help?

I no longer remember, though I think I did. Perhaps I only prayed thinking that it would help me accept whatever came. We pray for four reasons: petition, thanksgiving, repentance, and adoration. I would guess that most of my prayers from that day have been prayers of petition. I pray because I want something, a cure for Elie, health for my son Alexander, a job that would move us closer to family.

When I was younger, most of my prayers—what few I offered—were prayers of thanksgiving. I prayed in thankfulness and wonder for life and the creation around me, usually in summer and always outdoors. I prayed in the Adirondacks, steeped in mountains and clear streams. I prayed in the evening, at the foot of my bed with the warm summer breeze blowing in the window and the moon rising. I prayed in secret, not wanting to be seen with my head bowed. Often my prayer was not really prayer at all, but simply joy... joy and an unacknowledged inkling that the cause for that joy was something much bigger than the most immediate causes. Simple joy is a form of prayer, I think. Just as suffering is a form or prayer.

But now I often feel as if I only pray to receive something. I am a chronic petitioner, which makes me often feel as if I only turn to God when I am in need. I am a wealthy man if I count the riches of beautiful children and a loving wife. I live in a beautiful place, overlooking a bay of clean water on the north end of Lake Huron. I listen to the frogs in the evening. I have a front yard filled with flowers. An angelic saint lies quietly on my couch. Why do I not pray more often with thankfulness?

Something changes in us when we become parents. It changes the simple joy of living to the measured joy of caring and nurturing. My joy in my life and my children is always tempered now by the knowledge of its fragility. It is no longer possible to be carefree. As parents, we accept the total responsibility—with love—for another person's well-being and happiness. We ask for God's help in this. We petition because there is so much to beware. And sometimes in our care, we forget that the child whose life we have accepted as part of our own, is a beautiful manifestation of creation. The child is something for which to be supremely thankful. We are full of care because of our responsibility, but fail to see the joy that responsibility gives us.

~~~

At around 3 pm, it started to grow cool in the courtyard of Tisch Hospital. We moved back up to the ninth floor and the waiting area across from the room where we had spent our last night with Elie. Nobody spoke. Liz worried the Rosary in her hand. I stared out the window at the darkening courtyard. The hallway was dimly lit. People moved around the floor still, but quieted when they saw us. Liz told me a story that she had never told me before.

When we first came to the U.P. and Liz was pregnant with Elie, she was studying for a nursing degree. Her classes were in Sault Ste. Marie, about a 35 mile drive north of Cedarville. Going to and fro, Liz would always say the Rosary, often as an offering in the hopes of my conversion. One day, she decided to make a greater offering. From that day on, she prayed to God that she would accept any suffering if it would bring me to Catholicism.

She laughed sadly and turned to me. "As I was driving, I kept thinking that He would make me fat, or would give me acne or something." Then she became quiet. "I didn't want this," and she started to cry.

At around 3:30 pm, Dr. Epstein strode suddenly into the waiting area. He wore his surgical scrubs as always with his mask on top of his head. He reached his hand out and touched Liz's cheek. "I have some good news," he said. "Why don't we go sit down."

The news was almost all good. Dr. Wisoff was still closing Elie's skull, but the surgery seemed to have been remarkably successful. They were able to remove about 90% of the tumor. It was almost all gone. She had done very well, her signs were stable, and we would probably be able to see her in an hour or so.

The heaviness went out of the room. "Did you hear that?" Liz kept asking me. "Did you hear that? It's a miracle."

"Thank God," said Bette.

"It really is a miracle," said Frank. We were all laughing and hugging each other.

"I knew she was strong," I said. "I knew she could do this." The elation was incredible. "I can't wait to see her, that little darling," I said.

"Yes. I want to see her," said Liz.

It was a longer wait than we expected, but time passed quickly now. No one had eaten, so we decided to order take out and have it delivered while we waited to see Elie in the recovery room. My hunger had returned and, though my hands still shook, I was incredibly happy. Liz could not stop crying. She hugged her mother. My parents patted me on the shoulder. We talked about how we would now have to go through chemo, but how it didn't seem so bad anymore. The food arrived. I ate with gusto. Liz nibbled but still wasn't hungry. She wanted to see Elie. Families came into the waiting room smiling. Fathers shook my hands. "Congratulations," they told me. "We're so happy for you."

"We're praying for your little girl, too," Liz would say. "We're praying that it turns out as well."

"So are we," the parents said, worry showing behind their smiles. "We hope so."

And we would hug each other again, hug our parents, eat food, laugh about what a strong little girl Elie is.

"He said she might be blind," said Frank.

"It's a small thing," I said. "She's going to live, Frank."

"Maybe she won't be," said Bette. "He said she might not be. Only time will tell. We just have to keep praying."

What relief we all felt. What utter pouring out of fear, gushing out from us and across the floor, drifting away, dissipating. "I can't wait to hold her in my arms again," Liz sobbed, she was so happy. "I ache for her. My arms just ache."

"We'll see her soon," I smiled. "God is letting us keep her, I think."

"I know. Can you believe it?" She smiled, leaned back, and kissed my cheek. "I love you." It was such a tender moment, one of those moments when each spouse knows exactly what the other has felt, knows exactly how they think, a moment when they become one soul. "And I love our little girl," she added.

"I know that," I said laughing.

CHAPTER 11
Recovery

Two years later, I remembered that night on the ward. When I remembered it, Elie had then picked up a cold or flu and it caused her to sleep almost all the time. Her little body was strong then, but fighting infections and illness left her worn out. After a few days, we could hear the sickness moving from her sinuses down into her chest. Her breathing became shallow and very rapid, and when she coughed it was so weak that she couldn't loosen the phlegm in her throat. Liz and I took turns holding her in a steamy bathroom with the shower running for long stretches. We held her on our chests, carefully pounding her back to loosen the mucous. Finally, fearing pneumonia, Liz took her to the doctor. The illness turned out to be an ear infection in the early stages, which must have been causing some drainage and post-nasal drip. As soon as we started Elie on antibiotics, she began to sound better.

Every experience with illness serves to remind me: this could be the time. We could lose Elie now. We could lose her tomorrow. From the very moment when the doctors told us it was a brain tumor, we begged God not to take her from us just yet. Let us have her for a little while longer. Just through her first birthday. Then just through Christmas. Then Easter. Then another birthday.

The realization of how fleeting our time with her could be begs us to love her that much more carefully.

And what of God? He has given her to us. We have begged Him, many people have begged Him, and He has listened. He has given us the gift of time, waiting patiently until we are able to give Elie back to Him.

∽ ∾

The recovery room was on the floor above surgery. It is a room without windows, lit by veiled fluorescent bulbs and protected by mechanical doors marked red with tiny windows like portholes on a tug. The hallway is filled with gurneys and equipment, trash bags with used scrubs, a pile of towels. Visitors wait in the hall, call through on a red telephone, wait longer. The place has an unworldly feel to it, and through the windows, one sees the beds lined up, the orderlies moving quickly, the doctors checking patients, the nurses everywhere.

This is a place where nothing is certain, a post-operative limbo where things can easily go wrong. The patients are brought in unconscious. They are lined up with others, connected to monitors, checked very carefully by the nurses, watched over by the attending physician. Many are old, cardiac patients just out of bypass operations with monitors all over their chest. Some are conscious and sit up in their beds. Most are lying down, asleep.

I pick up the telephone in the hall and a nurse answers. She asks whom I want to see. I tell her. "Please wait." The line goes dead, and we linger along the wall. I look for Elie through the windows, but I can't find her in there. "Maybe she hasn't come down yet," I tell Liz. "I don't see a crib in there."

There are no seats in the hallway. We wait on a gurney pushed up against the wall. We wait a long time, and now time begins to pass very slowly. Other visitors come to the door, phone in, and are admitted without waiting. "Do you think something happened," Liz asks.

"I don't think so," I say, but I am not very sure of myself.

I call again, and the nurse tells me that Elie has just come down and they need to get her settled and hooked up to all of the monitors. It will just be a moment. Please be patient.

We go back to the gurney.

Two black women arrive—one older, one younger. They call in and are told to wait. They have Jamaican accents. I ask them whom they are waiting to see.

"My son, Christopher," the younger woman says. "He was operated on today." She is a heavy black woman with a charming smile. She asks us the same question, and we tell her about Elie and the tumor. She tells us about Chris's epilepsy. We both express our great optimism and the optimism of the surgeons. After a while the door opens and the two women are ushered in. Liz and I are still waiting.

After another ten minutes, Chris's mother and grandmother emerge. "He is well, God be praised," says the mother. "God be praised," echoes the grandmother.

"Did you see my little girl," I ask.

"We did," they say. "We couldn't get very close. They were around her crib, but she seems fine. She is sleeping. A very beautiful girl."

"Oh, God," says Liz, clutching her hands to her chest. "She is beautiful."

"Thank you," I say. "Thank you, thank you."

We wish each other good luck, and they head up to the waiting room by the ICU. We'll see each other again, I'm sure.

֍ ֍

They finally let us in after another thirty minutes. Elie was around the corner, in a metal bed with crib ends and a rail that they let down for us. We walked slowly toward her, trying to remain steady. I don't think anything could have prepared us for that moment, seeing her dwarfed on that large white bed, her tiny body naked, tubes coming out of everywhere, a white turban of gauze, a tube draining bloody fluid from her cranium. Liz almost collapsed at the sight.

"It's all right," I said. "She's alive. The surgery was a success." I held Liz's arm as we crossed the room, our eyes fixed on Elie's face. Her color was gone, her cheeks were pale, almost blue, like skimmed milk. She could have been dead, except for the sound of her labored breathing. The nurse explained that she was still in a somewhat critical condition and that she had received a pint of blood, which was a lot for an infant. She was lying on a bed of ice, crushed ice in a pack, wrapped in a towel.

"What is this," Liz asked

A nurse answered, "She has a post-operative fever. We need to try and get her temp down, so we've got the ice pack beneath her. She can't feel anything."

Liz started to shake. "Oh, my baby," she whispered.

"Is she in danger?" I asked.

"Of course," said the nurse, matter-of-factly. "She had a major surgery on her brain. A fever could be very dangerous if it gets too high. Plus the surgery was around the hypothalamus, which controls temperature regulation. She's doing as well as we would expect, though."

"Oh, God," Liz whispered to me. "I can't believe we did this to her."

I held Liz's hand.

We leaned down beside her bed, holding each other's hands. Liz's fingernails were white as she gripped my arm. Our elbows rested on the covers beside Elie. We talked to her, we stroked her hand, we kissed her on her nose and told her how much we wanted to pick her up. Elie's face had never been more angelic, her features never more diminutive.

Liz cried and the tears dripped on the sheet beside Elie. I tried to sing to her. I cannot remember anything we said.

After a few moments it seemed as if her breathing grew more labored. The attending nurse kept trying to readjust the oxygen sensor attached to Elie's big toe. It was reading O_2 levels around 70% to 80%. The attending doctor moved our way.

"I don't like the O_2 readings," the nurse said.

"Switch the pickup to her thumb," the attending said.

"I love you Elie," Liz was cooing in Elie's ear. "I love my little girl. She's a good girl. Can you hear me sweetie-pie? Do you know your mommy is here?"

The nurse was working around us. I was aware of what they were doing. I read the instruments as they worked, but could only sense the danger from their urgency. Elie's breathing was very audible. "Is she all right?" I asked the nurse.

"Her oxygen saturation is low," she replied. "A lot of times it's the machines. I'm going to switch the pickup."

"Kent, isn't she the most beautiful thing?"

"I love her," I said, looking at the tube that drained blood from her head and realizing everything that she had been through. "Stay with us, Elie. Be our little girl."

Patients in recovery are so carefully tended precisely because things can happen fast. It is as if the body waits around while the soul decides if it wants to return. It could so easily part at this point. The nurses and doctors are all trained to respond. The equipment is immediately available. The mood is always tense. The surprise comes because, as a parent who has just heard wonderful news about the success of an operation, one never expects to see the emergency.

Elie's breathing got suddenly very difficult. Her chest began to heave, as if she couldn't breathe. Her body arched back. The nurse called out and others surrounded the bed immediately. Liz began crying. "Elie. Oh, baby. My baby. Please Elie. My baby, please."

A nurse pulled us back. "What's happening?" I asked, "What's the matter?"

"Post-operative trauma," she said. "The doctors need room now to work. I need to ask you to step back. Go outside while we get everything stabilized."

Liz was sobbing, her hands held out to Elie. "My baby. Oh, my baby," she kept saying. She just wanted to pick her up and protect her. Elie's breathing was loud and abrasive, as if she were trying to squeeze air through a nearly closed hole.

"Please step out," the nurse said, as she guided us forcefully away. "She's in good hands. We'll call you in again when she is more stable. It will probably be twenty to thirty minutes."

Liz was sobbing. Her head hung down and she leaned heavily on my arm. I tried to guide her out, but she could barely walk. "I want her back," she murmured. "Oh, my baby. I just... want.... to... hold her."

We stepped out through the mechanical doors, and I led Liz to the elevator. I wanted to get her up to the waiting room with our families. I was afraid she might collapse on the floor in a sudden breakdown. Her arms were shaking violently. Her chest heaved with the sobbing. She was bent over nearly double and would suddenly lash out and smash her fists against her thighs. "I didn't mean to do this," she sobbed. "I didn't want to do this to her."

"It's all right, Liz. We're going upstairs now," I said. "We'll say the Rosary with your family."

"I don't care. I don't care. I DON'T CARE," she smashed her hands against her thighs. "I just want Elie. I... want.... my... baby."

I managed to get Liz to the waiting room again. She seemed delirious. We sat down with our families around us. Liz couldn't answer any questions. Her head rolled around in a circle. She rocked back and forth. Her hands rubbed each other awkwardly. She moaned aloud.

"It wasn't good," I said. "She had trouble breathing." Our parents were touching us. My father was crying.

"ICE," Liz shouted suddenly. "SHE'S NAKED!" she screamed, then went back to rocking, rolling her head around disjointedly. "Oh. Oh. My baby. Oh." She hit the chair with the palms of her hand. Bette knelt down beside Liz and cradled her head. "She's dying and I can't hold her," Liz said.

"I'm going back down," I said. "Take care of Liz. I've got to be there in case anything happens." I turned the corner and ran for the elevator.

⊰ ⊱

The next hour was the most terrible in my life. They made me wait outside the doors for at least thirty minutes. I could just see the foot of Elie's bed through one of the windows, and I could see the movement of doctors and nurses around it. Things had calmed somewhat, but there was still a crowd around her. I called in repeatedly, but the nurse told me to wait again and again. I asked if she was all right, and the nurse responded that she was, but that I would have to wait.

I did not really think that Elie was dying. The breathing had been terrible. It sounded like she was dying, but the doctors had said the operation was good. It didn't seem likely to me that she was dying. I waited and thought about how my life had changed so suddenly, without any inkling of the years ahead and how different they would be from what I had expected. At each point, at each downturn, we were both very innocent, ignorant of the demands these changes would place on us. We were always aware of the present, the problem at hand. To our way of thinking at that time, the result was either good or bad. Elie either survived and was better, or died and was lost to us. It never occurred to us that the real result would be somewhere between the two.

After a half hour, I slipped in a set of doors around the corner that were used to bring patients out of the recovery room and up to ICU. The doors were just around the corner from Elie's bed. I stood about 15 yards away and watched the work. I could see her small face, her features calm again. I could see her chest rise and fall with her rapid, light breaths. She had calmed.

I hovered at the exit, an unwelcome visitor. Staff moved around me without notice, assuming I had been allowed in. I was afraid to move to Elie's bed because they would send me out again. I just wanted to see her, to watch over her, even if it was from a distance. Not being there if something were to happen would be the worst thing of all, but not being strong enough to simply approach her bedside because it was my right as her father seemed weak as well. She was my daughter. If I could not tell nurses and doctors to go to hell and that I was going to be there next to her no matter what happened, then I was just weak.

I would face that dilemma again in future, but the sense of my failure would be far stronger. When Liz and I met Pope John Paul II, and I had a few, brief moments to ask for what I most wanted but did not, the lingering sense of failure as a father was and remains strong.

At these few times, as father, as protector, I have been torn between wanting to do anything possible to help my child and wanting to hold back because of a fear of... of what? Of being wrong in my convictions about what was right? Of being unable to stand my ground against authority? Of fearing my own failure as a father? A failure to protect as I should, and so yielding up my responsibility to others? Or simply a failure of my own faith? A weakness of my faith and an unwillingness to trust completely. Sometimes I wonder if I have not written this book to understand my own faith, or lack of it. Perhaps that is at the heart of my search, the core of what Elie is trying to teach me.

∽ ∾

The land around my home was rolling farms and rounded hills when I was growing up. It was pastures fitted into woods, grassy verges to the roads, meadows beneath the power lines. Everywhere one looked as we moved through that landscape there was a field rising up a hill and over the top, framed in by maple and beech woods.

I was captivated by that image as a boy—the field stretching over the hill. I was intrigued by the other side, by what lay beyond vision, the next field over, the hidden pasture. And the thought of going to see it was a recurrent daydream for me. In successive years, the method of travel changed. One summer I dreamed of owning a horse, of riding the horse over the hill, through the next field, over the hill beyond that, through the Finger Lakes to the southern tier, and from there into the Appalachian mountains to a place where few people lived, where life was simple and raw.

Another summer, I would go in my daydream by motocross bike. Load up, pack a duffle on the back, ride up the margin of the field and over the hill. Still another I dreamed of flying an ultralight. I even took flying lessons, learned about ultralights, schemed about ways to afford buying one, measured the cul-de-sac on my street for takeoff length.

Where was I always trying to go? The field over the hill. It never really changed for me, and, in truth, I never really had any sense of what was over the backside. Rather it was the image of the unknown. Over the top was a mystic place, a place of hidden beauty, cultivated yet with no sign of the cultivator, a secret place that I would enter alone. The beauty of the image for me was the journey that accompanied it, the sense of being willing to set forth into the unknown.

Sigurd Olson said, "Life is a series of open horizons, with one no sooner completed than another looms ahead... Penetrations into the unknown, all give meaning to what has gone before and courage for what is to come. More than physical features they are horizons of mind and spirit... And when there are no longer any beckoning mirages ahead a man dies."

Yet death itself has become something like that distant mirage for me. Sometimes the sun sets beneath clouds and the resulting fiery red and blue imprint on the sky is like a heavenly landscape stretching into eternity. The clouds become distant hills disappearing into a blue mist. Perhaps that is the landscape we venture toward in death. If that were true, I don't think I would mind dying. It is my field over a hill, stretched out into eternity.

My living with Elie dying has made me view death differently. I am in no rush, but I wonder if it will finally allow me to make my journey. I will simply walk over the hill. The thought no longer frightens me.

And there is another daydream that often comforts me.

I imagine the moment when I will come before the throne of God with the angels surrounding Him. And for all my sins, still there, at God's feet, will be a little girl with straight blond hair who will look at me, hold out a hand in welcome, and say, "Hi Daddy. Do you want to see what I've been doing all this time?"

CHAPTER 12
Time Flies

I pause for breath and find I look out on a July evening and already another two years have passed between finishing those words and beginning these. They pass in an instant, and I am the richer by three children, twin boys—now two years old and an infant girl, Hannah.

The rhythm of life speeds up as I age. Perhaps it is simply one of life's cadences, a rallentando that carries us toward a finale.

But perhaps it has to do with memory. We have a set number of distinguishable moments in life, and I know that a growing proportion of the moments which I possess in memory are given over to care and anxiety for my young family.

When we are young, we have few cares. Life is full of experiences, freshness, vigor, infatuation, epiphany. The moments of our youth are highlighted by sunshine and stand out in memory as a flood of events, each one partially remembered—or, if not exactly remembered, at least filed away, taking up space in the closet of our brain. And that filled space is something of which we are aware. It is like memory if it is not memory itself.

The moments of worry for a boy, a student, a young college man were scattered showers in a glory of summer days. Falling in love, finding a wife, exploring life with a new and lovely other person—these were all new as well.

But that changes as we age. The proportion given over to care and worry grows, and moments dominated by worry are indistinguishable from each other. Each moment of worry is like every other. Taken together, they become lost to memory. They become like a grey haze that hangs over memory, that obscures it, the pollution of our emotional landscape. They fill no space in our minds because they have no relief.

The interstices of pleasure, sadness, joy, heartache become punctuation marks that stand out in memory, sharp heartbeats of vivid rock in a desert landscape wind-scoured by care and concern. These memorable events are ever fewer and further between. It is as if we walk through that vivid landscape, but spend ever more time looking at the ground to ensure we do not fall. Our view, our memory is of the stones in our path, not the landscape around us. The few times that we feel safe to look up are splendid, but these become compressed in time because they are surrounded by an empty sameness. And time seems to speed by faster when we look back.

∽ ∼

We expected to lose Elie this past June. We were prepared to lose her.

We've been prepared before, Liz and I, but this time somehow we were more prepared. We expected it. It seemed to me as I looked into her half-open eyes and her pale, almost bluish cheeks that Elie was ready, that Elie almost willed it. And as I thought about her, listened to her sharp, terribly sad cries from a pain of no source we could identify, I willed it. I wanted it to be over for Elie. Hasn't she suffered enough? Must this be prolonged?

I knew when I could ask those questions, I was ready to accept her death. But it did not come.

We talked to our doctors—multiple doctors—about how to comfort Elie. We tested and retested her for illnesses, infections, kidney stones, head pressure, appendicitis, ear infections, liver problems, renal failure. We identified pancreatitis at one point and spent a week in the hospital, only to find once she was released and sent home that she had gastritis. We treated that, but the pain continued. It seemed constant and horrible.

Our doctors finally agreed that she was in the final stages of life and that Elie's system was simply shutting down. We all had tried so hard to find ways to help her. One day, our neurologist suggested giving regular morphine to comfort her. He told us her time was limited in that state. Days or weeks.

Our pediatrician, a wonderful man, was more circumspect. He understood our hesitancy to use morphine and potentially hasten Elie's death, and he knew the depth of Liz's faith. He suggested we use morphine if we felt she needed it, but also suggested we could use it more sparingly. He said we should try to give her a chance to recover if that was possible. "It is such a difficult choice," he said.

We followed his advice. Our families prayed for Elie, but Elie got worse and we were giving her morphine every night for four days. During the day, she cried and jerked her right arm involuntarily, her clearest expression of pain. After four days, we knew she was likely to become addicted to the morphine soon. Once that happened, we worried we would not be able to pull her off because the pain of withdrawal symptoms from opiates would be indistinguishable from her other pain. It would lead to constant morphine, and the morphine would eventually cause her to stop breathing.

We asked a local priest to visit her and administer Last Rites. Father Halloran is an older priest who retired years ago to a small piece of forest down the lake. He still says Mass each Sunday and visits the sick regularly. We talked for a long while about Elie. He asked us questions, and then he anointed her. During the prayer he turned to Liz and me and said, "You know it may not be in God's plan for Elie to be healed, but we can ask God to be merciful and to give us strength in what we have to face. And we can ask God to give Elie peace."

After the priest left, Liz made the sign of the cross on Elie's forehead with a bottle of holy water we brought from Lourdes six years ago. The water is in a plastic coke bottle that we cleaned out in Lourdes and has remained under our sink in one house or another since then. I pick it up every now and then and wonder that it hasn't developed its own ecosystem. But it is still as clear as the day we filled it.

That night Elie had the first night without pain for two months. She slept eight hours and when she awoke, she was as happy as I have ever seen her.

∽ ∾

There have been three times that we felt sure Elie was dying. This last was the closest we have yet come. Before that, we were in a hospital with a stomach problem, severe protein deficiency, and a dangerous infection. The time before that, only a year after her surgery, she went to sleep one afternoon and didn't wake up for five days.

When she finally awoke, lying in her mother's arms in a hammock by the lake, her right eye would not open. It remained closed for a week in a perpetual wink, as if her body weren't quite ready to give up the coma that her spirit had quit. Then, one day, her eye opened as well.

I have given up trying to predict or understand these periods. Her health rolls on, sometimes up, sometimes down. When it is down, it goes way down, yet her resilience is astonishing.

Still, whenever she gets sick, I wonder if this is the time. Is this the illness that will finally overwhelm her frail body? Elie, I really believe, wants to live, but she is being betrayed by her body.

∽ ∾

In the evening I play music at the piano. We brought an old upright all the way back to New York from Michigan, where I had purchased it from Mary, one of Elie's nurses, for $75. She was a lovely Mexican nurse who joined us when we first took Elie back to Michigan. Her husband is an artist who does vivid watercolors of southwestern and Mexican traditional pottery. They decided after two winters in Michigan to return to southern Texas.

At $75, it was probably a dubious investment, but it played well enough that I could again take up an instrument that I had started learning at nineteen and always loved.

I am not the lightest touch on a piano, but by the time we brought it all the way East in a U-Haul, it had become so brassy sounding that Liz used to take the twins up to her room so that she did not have to listen to me play.

Two winters ago, I decided to fix it and bought a book on piano reconditioning. It took a full winter and, in the meantime, I borrowed some money from my parents and bought a beautiful Steinway grand for our living room.

Still, I finished rebuilding the working internals and refinishing the wood, and it came out remarkably well. So we moved it down to Elie's room, and now I can play to her in the evenings when we have no nurse and the other children are playing with their toys around her.

We play classical, ragtime, rock and roll. Sometimes we sing together—me playing a poor piano and Liz singing off-key.

And I believe Elie has come to expect the music. Her teachers at school say now that when they play a tape of piano music at school, Elie turns her head to it. She certainly does that when I play in her room. If she is upset or tired of sitting in one position, I will switch her and then play music, and she almost always calms down, relaxes, and rolls her eyes around.

Various doctors have made a point of telling us that Elie cannot be aware, that she is a "vegetable"—a descriptive term that we hate, or that she is in "a persistent vegetative state"—a medical term that I hate even more.

They are wrong. Elie is alive and aware. She is a person. She loves, she longs, she tries within the strict limitations of her condition to communicate. She does communicate. Her nurses know it. We know it. Sometimes, perhaps more often than not, those who know how to listen understand her.

And when I sit and play a Beethoven sonatina on Elie's rebuilt piano, I know that she knows something about pleasure and about the joy of life.

CHAPTER 13
Purgatory

Our time in the hospital was long, nearly seven weeks, and many of the days blur together in memory such that when I look back, I remember only a few highlights, a few moments of real happiness. Much more, I am awed by the depth of our ignorance, which in itself was a sort of blessing.

Elie lay abed and did not wake for nearly a week. She wore only a diaper because of her fever, and she was bandaged in a turban with a drainage tube coming from the top of her skull. Liz and I sat patiently around her, stroked her hand, talked to her. The surgeons stopped by once or twice a day. They smiled at me, ruffled Liz's hair, said, "Hang in there kiddo." And we did. We thought everything was good.

I believe now that our surgeons knew something had gone seriously wrong with the operation in the first few days, probably even the second day when Elie did not regain consciousness. Nobody told us—or they told us very slowly when they could no longer not tell us. But it was never direct.

I remember telling the doctor that she had yawned in her sleep and looking at him as if to imply that it was a hopeful sign, it meant she would soon wake.

"I don't know," he said, and added slowly, "Yawning is a reflexive action. It has nothing to do with consciousness."

He knew. He had watched so many children through these first few critical hours, and he knew they were supposed to wake up. Barring complications, they should wake up. But he was not sure, and he did not want to explain a frightening reality to two parents living on hope.

Our room looked over the East River at the Citgo sign and Brooklyn. Across the river were the four stacks of a power plant, further out the tall, blue Citibank building. Cars whizzed by continually on the FDR highway, heading uptown.

Friends stopped by, couples we knew from college, none of whom had had children yet. Other single friends came and brought pizza. My dad came often because he had moved into a hotel on 37th and Lexington to handle a corporate sale and could pop over easily early in the morning or at the end of his long days. I often sent him out to 28th and 3rd for take-out Indian food. Sometimes I left him with Elie while Liz slept and went for food myself, just needing to spend some time in a world outside of the hospital. I would wander down 3rd, turn up toward Washington Square, find myself in a lovely little courtyard with a private park and brownstones around it with small, brass marquees announcing movie studios or recording companies. I would sit on a bench along the high fence in a slant of sun and just try to reinvigorate myself, build up the strength to go back to the hospital and spend another night there.

I worried about my job. I had been with my company for two years. Normally, I worked out of an office alone, hours from our state office in Lansing. I wondered if the time stretched on here whether they would eventually have to let me go. I worried about our health benefits. I had to keep those. I could not lose my job. How would we take care of Elie?

I remember calling my supervisor once from Ann Arbor when we decided to take Elie back to New York. I told him that Elie had a brain tumor. I could barely get the words out, but I said that we wanted to take her back to New York. We couldn't stay in the U.P. with her. I promised I would come back as soon as I could. "Look," I said, "I'm worried if you will still want me in this job." It was so hard to say for me because I've never cared before about losing a job, but this one suddenly I cared immensely about.

"Kent," Bill said to me, "that should be the last thing on your mind. I will figure out how to get you leave. We'll use your sick time. You use your vacation. I'll try to get some additional administrative leave (he ended up getting me an extra month with pay). Then you can go on unpaid leave. There will be a job here for you. Don't worry about that."

I was as grateful to him as I have ever been to anyone.

∽ ↷

Liz never left the hospital, with one exception, when we dressed up and went on an abbreviated date to see La Bohéme at Lincoln Center. She stayed with Elie round the clock, slipping out for a few hours to an adjoining room that the hospital set aside for parents. She would only leave if I was there. Once we were out of ICU and back on the floor, she often lay in the crib with Elie, curled up around our child, with her toes sticking through the metal bars of the crib, fast asleep. She held Elie, rocked her back and forth, kissed her, talked to her, changed her diapers. Thank God we were so young then and that Elie was our first. It would be so hard to do now.

She and I had such different ways of dealing with this time. She extinguished her self and her own wants. She simply existed to nurture Elie. She visited other children on our floor with Elie in a stroller, talked to other mothers. But the outside world did not exist, and so she had no desire to leave the hospital. She knew her place as strongly as she has ever known anything.

I found an increasing need to spend time away. I was plagued by worries about my job, about our health benefits, about our finances. The world did exist. It was moving past us as if we were a knife blade in the current of a river. As a week stretched into two, and then three, I grew restless. I called my boss one night at his home. It was late, probably ten o'clock, but I had no idea of the time. Time sort of disappeared in the hospital.

"Hi, Bill."

"Kent?"

"Yeah. Listen, I was thinking. Maybe we could buy the property out on Point Brulee. I never told you, but the owner stopped by my office a few days before I left. They might sell all 300 acres to us."

"Oh. Uh-huh."

I think back now on the phone call with a mixture of embarrassment and laughter. I was so desperate to deal with something besides death and disease. I just wanted to talk to someone about anything else, and work was best. I can see Bill, sitting on his couch next to his wife, watching TV in the dark, dozing. My call startles him awake. We talk. He hangs up. Jane asks Bill who it was. He tells her.

"What did he want?"

"I don't know," Bill says bemusedly. "I have no idea."

After about three weeks, I asked Liz's uncle if I could use his apartment during the day to do some work. He lived in a high-rise at 89th and Madison. His balcony looked out over Central Park. He had a stationary bike set up in a spare room. He had a desk and a phone. He gave me a key, and I started going up there every morning for five or six hours at first, more later on.

I did work there. I called landowners, looked for parcels of land we could buy, talked to people in the National Forest about tracts they wanted, wrote letters to absentee landowners. I don't know if anything I did there ever produced a single thing for us. I can't remember. I just needed to work on something, to do more than simply wait.

And whenever I returned to the hospital at the end of an afternoon, Liz was there with Elie, smiling, welcoming me back, telling me the little things Elie had done. How she had stretched today. The big yawn she had made. The frightened seizure and the crying she had done. It all seemed like progress to us.

✧ ✧

As I look back, the thing that surprises me most about that first week in the ICU was the amount we reached out to others around us. Our child lay still, unconscious, naked on her back. All around us lay children and parents, mostly mothers, who were involved in various tragedies.

The Jamaican mother and grandmother were next to us with their boy, Christopher. Although only four, he was as large as an eight-year old. Tall, with long, lanky, black legs and pink-soled feet. He lay, gangly in the bed, a beautiful, big boy. The first night we heard him calling, "Daddy. Daddy."

It was such a longing cry. Liz slipped over when he was sleeping to talk to the mother. "Poor kid, he wants his father," she said.

"Yes," the woman said. "His dad was a taxi driver. One week ago, he was shot by some kids who robbed him. Chris saw it on the evening news. He called me into the room saying 'Mommy... Daddy's car is on the news.'"

"My God," Liz gasped.

The woman was dry-eyed, almost matter-of-fact, as if murder was something expected, normal. "I don't think he really understood, but he wants his dad now."

Liz returned and told me the story behind our curtain in a hushed whisper. We both sat in our uncomfortable chairs, hugging our knees and crying every time we heard Christopher call out for his dad that night.

Within a day or two, we knew all of the stories on the ward. Liz moved from station to station, talking to the other mothers, sharing our story, listening to theirs. Such desperation.

The woman across from us sat beside her three year-old boy. They had come all the way from Texas because Fred Epstein was the only surgeon who would operate on his spinal tumors. She had already lost one child from the same disease. Her parents were with her.

The boy in the bed, Ryan, was a sweet, quiet kid with straight, brown bangs. He slept a lot, but when he was awake, he talked about going to Disneyworld.

His mother looked shell-shocked. She hardly spoke. Sometimes she almost seemed catatonic. Ryan was her second child to suffer from brain and spinal tumors. She lost her first boy two years before. Liz learned that this was Ryan's second surgery and they had found a dozen new metastases on his spine and brain stem. The mother knew she was going to lose Ryan the same as her first. Her husband had left her two weeks before Ryan's second surgery, walked out on her and left his child to die without him. The grandparents were just hoping Ryan would live long enough that they could contact Make-a-Wish Foundation and bring him to Disneyworld.

Their suffering was crushing. Liz spent a lot of time trying to talk to the mother and help her, but more talking to Ryan—a surrogate mother for him to talk to and hold his hand when his real mother lay curled in the armchair next to him, eyes open but unresponsive.

Liz was amazing this way. There was such need in the room around us, and with her spontaneous joyfulness, she filled that need for some people. We were wide-eyed. We had no idea what wrenching decisions we faced. We thought we were lucky—we **were** lucky—and we tried to give others some of our sense of hope.

The hardest case I saw in the ICU was a tiny baby girl who came in without a parent. She was at most five or six pounds and had had open heart surgery for a defect. She lay in the bed crying quite often during the day with no one to hold or comfort her. The nurses took care of her as best they could, but were too busy to rock her, cuddle her, play with her hands. She was all alone there.

While Elie was still unconscious, Liz would go sit by the baby and stroke her arm or leg. She was black as night with a mop of tight curls and tiny features. Her cry was small but piteous.

One afternoon I heard our chief resident, a woman our age, complaining angrily to the nurse next to her, "What does she think this is, a charity ward. She just brings her in here and drops her off and expects us to take care of her. She should be over at Bellevue. We'll have to transfer her soon." I realized they were talking about the baby.

Late that night, the mother came in. She was obviously a poor, black immigrant—Haitian or Dominican or something. She never looked up at anyone, but she fussed over the baby, efficiently and with real care. She changed her, she cuddled her. After about an hour, she laid her back in the bed and left.

At the time, I thought she was probably a working, single mom. She came in on a Friday night when she could, but couldn't come any other times. Later, I began to wonder if the mother had not stayed away on purpose. She knew her child needed surgery. She knew if she was left at NYU she would be cared for there. A hospital could not just turn a critically ill child out. Perhaps there was even a rule about providing urgent care.

Bellevue was the hospital for the poor. It was two blocks down, and just looking at the outside on my walks, I could see that it would not be the place I would choose for my child. Perhaps the mother left her child on purpose, placing her faith in God that her daughter would get the treatment she needed at the better hospital. If the mother showed up, they might make her take the baby away or transfer her. If she didn't show up, they could not do anything.

The following morning, the baby was gone. While we slept in our chairs, the baby and mother had left. I asked about her at the central desk in the morning. For some reason the little baby and the chief resident's comments had really gotten under my skin. I knew I would do exactly the same thing as the mother had done if I were in her position. The resident seemed to assume the mother did not care for her child. I assumed the opposite. The mother loved her child, but the health care system in which she found herself did not particularly love or value her.

A shameful truth of our health system is that if you are poor, you get much worse care than if you are well off. But the greater truth is that a mother's love can find ways to protect the child from even the most perverse system.

Two days later, I wandered across to Bellevue on one of my walks. I wanted to see the baby again.

Parts of the hospital were shocking. Everything seemed dingy. Water stains marked the ceiling tiles, plaster falling down in places, the floors dirty. The place seemed to be run by med students and residents, and I later heard—though I don't know if it is true—that many of the NYU residents pulled rotations at the city hospital to keep it running in addition to their regular rotations at Tisch.

I found the juxtaposition of a hospital that was clearly filled with the best doctors, equipment, and facilities right next door to one that exuded poverty somehow shocking. Care for those with means next to much worse care for those without.

I wandered the halls and inquired at the ICU desk in Bellevue, but I never found the little girl or her mother.

∽ ∾

The neuro-surgeon in residence was a nice, young Korean named Kim. He seemed extremely competent, and with him we set aside our general rule to ignore anything that residents told us. We listened carefully when he visited. He came regularly, two or three times a day, while the surgeon in charge showed for morning or evening rounds only.

One afternoon, Dr. Kim came in with recent CT scans. He flicked on a light for the viewer within our area of the ICU and pushed two sets of X-rays up under the clamps.

"I want to show you the changes we've seen to Elizabeth's brain in the last 48 hours," he began.

"These latest scans don't look all that good. What you are looking at in this first image is the top of the head as if it were sliced off. There is plenty of healthy tissue. It's light grey," he said, pointing to the parts of the brain.

"Now go down deeper into the brain. In the scan just after surgery, it is all healthy tissue." He pointed out the cysts, the tumor, the healthy brain.

"Now look at the most recent image. This same cross-section shows much of the brain in both lobes as a darker grey."

He looked up at me meaningfully, but said nothing.

"What does that mean," I asked.

He hesitated. The dark grey indicates necrotic tissue. It's dead."

He looked at me again and waited. I stared at the pictures. It was hard to see the difference, but if you looked carefully enough it was there.

"I'm not sure I understand," I said. "It looks to me like most of her brain is that way."

"Yes," he said. "There has been a tremendous amount of damage. We believe your daughter had a stroke, probably after surgery." Long pause.

He went on, "The arteries and capillaries in the brain are tiny, and sometimes in spite of the medication we put on them, the vessels can spasm after handling. If that happens, the blood supply can be cut off and the affected brain dies."

I looked at Liz, not really sure what this meant. She had been quiet the whole time. Finally she spoke.

"I thought the surgery was a success," she said.

"Mmmm," Dr. Kim said, putting his knuckle to his front teeth and raising an eyebrow. He looked straight into Liz's eyes. "It was successful in the sense that we got the tumor mostly," he said, "but the stroke is clearly not a good result."

"What does this mean for Elie," I asked. "What will she be like?"

He shifted feet and looked directly into my eyes. "I don't know," he said, "but many of the primary motor areas are in the necrotic sites. Speech, movement, memory... all these are affected."

"However," he went on, "a child's brain before two to four years is very plastic. If some tissue dies, it is possible for the brain to create new pathways that recapture the needed skills. We've known children with half their brain removed who were able to recover largely and lead very normal lives. You might find it difficult to pick someone like that out if you passed them on the street."

His voice trailed off. We all stood there in the ICU, looking at each other. Neither Liz nor I said anything. We did not really understand what he had told us.

After a few minutes, he said, "At this point, we really don't know. At the very least it will mean a lot of rehabilitative therapy, but it is extremely fortunate that she is so young. There is a lot of hope for children who undergo brain damage."

CHAPTER 14
Lourdes

Forty-two days after we entered the hospital with Elie, we left again to take her home to our family on Long Island.

It was a difficult decision to leave the hospital. We wanted more than anything to be in our own home, to sleep in our own bed, to care for Elie with all of her family around her. At the same time, we wanted to remain in the safety of a hospital, watched over by the nurses, surrounded by the other families who could share an understanding of what we were facing. There was strength in the community of intense anxiety which made up the children's cancer floor at the hospital.

The decision was more difficult still because Elie had not really improved much. She was awake, but unresponsive. She cried a lot, but gave no indication that she was aware of us at all. She stiffened in a series of primitive reflexes that we called posturing. She had terrible difficulty with her feedings. Most frightening of all, she threw up suddenly and often.

In one visit with a doctor, we asked in a moment of interlude during his examination what was likely to be Elie's fate. He answered, very matter-of-factly, that children like Elie usually aspirated and died of pneumonia. It was hard to keep their lungs safe because they were so compromised already. In addition to her tumor now, she was unable to move. She had lost her gag reflex. She couldn't roll over if she were to vomit. All it would take was one time and she would get pneumonia, with pneumonia after pneumonia following. We still very much looked for improvement over time and with therapy, but it was going to be a long, hard fight to get Elie beyond this dangerous period.

Liz and I talked about it that night at the hospital. We agreed that we would care for her so that she would not end up in a series of declining pneumonias. We prayed again together and asked God not to take our only child.

The goal which moved us beyond the fear of leaving the safety of the hospital was the desire to bring Elie to Lourdes. We had postponed a trip to Lourdes when Fred Epstein and Jeff Wisoff had given us hope that Elie's tumor could be removed. That ray of hope had jarred the composure we had gained through the acceptance of Elie's fate. We had been resigned to the tumor being untreatable, but we had planned to make a pilgrimage to ask God for a miracle. Lourdes remained, after the surgery and the dawning realization that perhaps Elie was more in need of a miracle than ever, a goal that Liz and I talked about late that night in the hospital. We wondered if a trip was possible, and how we would ever be able to take Elie with all of her medicines, feeding pumps and other equipment.

We asked Liz's mother what she thought, and she offered to come with us. We would be three adults with one child. That made it seem possible.

The days in the hospital lengthened out to five weeks. Elie was out of intensive care, and we had been living in a shared room with a young black girl and her parents. She was four and had advanced leukemia. Her mother and father were friendly, but living in a small room together was very difficult. As we began hearing intimations about us going home, I started making plans.

We could have left after five weeks. Liz and I had both mastered the feeding pumps and the medicine regime. In fact, for the last two weeks, we provided total care to Elie, and the floor nurses did very little beyond bringing the required medicines at the appointed time. We often reminded them if something was late. Liz was becoming a very competent nurse herself.

But as the "last" week unfolded, Liz began to worry. It was easy taking care of Elie in the hospital because there was a safety net. Elie seemed very unpredictable. Her temperature might go up one day and down the next. She would have a frightening startle seizure without warning or might go into a period of serial vomiting. We could handle all of these things, but we knew that if we had questions or didn't know what to do, it was easy to ask and get help. The thought of being completely on our own was frightening. We barely knew how to take care of a normal child. We were at sea with a severely sick child. Liz decided to stay another week.

Leaving the hospital to go home was hard. Taking Elie to Lourdes was a leap of faith. There, we would really be on our own. We could count on no backup and no emergency options. There would be a doctor in an emergency there, but we would have all the problems of translation, explaining her condition, securing alternative medicines if she needed them. If going to Lourdes seemed like climbing to the top of a long flight of stairs, taking Elie out of the hospital and back to Liz's home in New York was the first step up.

The amazing thing is that the extra week Liz tagged on because of our uncertainty was crucial in the long run to supporting Elie at home. Eventually, we needed nursing support to care for her. The only way to afford it was through a Medicaid program in New York that provides help for families to care for severely disabled children at home instead of in a hospital or institution. As one of the measures of need, the program had a fairly arbitrary eligibility criterion of forty-one days in the hospital. More than forty-one and your child was considered hard enough to care for that you could get nursing help. Less than forty-one days and support from the program was much more difficult to obtain.

At the time, we knew nothing about this. In fact, we had no idea that we would or could have nurses at home to help care for Elie. The last week, however, became very important a year later. Elie left the hospital on June 26, forty-two days after she entered.

Ten days later we left for Lourdes.

∽ ∾

Liz and I had spent six weeks inside a hospital. We had been through a harrowing emotional experience. We lost Elie in Ann Arbor with the first news. We regained her with the chance visit to Epstein and Wisoff. We lost her in a way that we didn't fully understand yet on the operating table. We wondered if we would regain her again over time.

We wore those six weeks in our visages. Looking back at pictures now, I see two pained, stretched, pallid faces. Our complexions look translucent, slightly jaundiced. Our eyes are weary. We have set smiles, but not far behind those smiles is a cup brimming with pain, frustration, some part of denial and a terrible sadness. Yet we remained optimistic. I think again as I look at the pictures that one of our best defenses was our ignorance. The future was unknown, and we had hope.

That was the driving force behind our visit to Lourdes. It filled us with a sense of hope. Clearly we both hoped for the miracle of miracles—to see Elie rise up healed from the baths of Lourdes, to hear her voice, to see her smile. Yet our need drove far deeper than that. We had ourselves to fill as well. The depth to which we had drawn down our own emotional and spiritual reserves to endure the past six weeks and to give everything we could to Elie had left us with an empty space in ourselves. Lourdes was our chance to fill it.

I was very concerned about money at that point. I was earning a small salary—somewhere in the low thirties. We had no extra money to spend. Since returning to the states from Oxford, Liz and I had been vegetarians, in part because we could not afford meat. We pinched and saved wherever we could, and the cost of a trip to Lourdes was beyond our means. I scoured the *New York Times* for low-priced tickets, but it still seemed beyond us.

During the six weeks since we returned to New York from Michigan, we had received hundreds of cards and letters. I think at least half of the families in Cedarville sent us notes. Friends from college sent letters or cards, particularly to Liz. We had letters from strangers who were friends of our friends. One was from a woman in Minnesota whose prayer chain had put Elie at the top of their prayers. Her group included hundreds of people from all over the country. Another was from a family in Chicago. We kept all of the notes, and they fill three large boxes.

Two letters in particular stand out with regard to Lourdes. The first was from our friends Anthony and Laurence, whom we had known at Oxford. Anthony was from Vancouver, studying climate modeling. Laurence was a beautiful French woman from Toulouse, studying the economics of rice production in Africa. They sent us an invitation to their wedding, which was planned for the town of Vielle-Aure, near the Spanish border in the Pyrenees. The wedding date was the end of July. I looked on a map. Vielle-Aure was 50 miles from Lourdes. Liz and I talked offhand of making our Lourdes trip at the same time as the wedding and going to see all of our friends from Oxford, who were traveling to the wedding en masse. We both thought of it as something of a pipe dream since there were so many reasons we would not be able to travel.

The second letter arrived during the last few days that we were in the hospital. It was from our friends Debbie and Scott. We had talked to various friends about possibly taking Elie to Lourdes, but we had usually talked about it in an offhand way. It seemed unrealistic. The letter had a short note from Debbie that said only, "For Lourdes." It enclosed a check for $500. To me it was the most surprising and generous gift because it came like an answer to a prayer. Debbie and Scott are not Catholic, so Lourdes meant little to them except that they knew how important it was to Liz. After they sent us the money, they never said anything about it again—I think they were too gentle to ever want us to feel in their debt. Yet I do, because they recognized that we really needed something and they provided it as they could. It was the sort of gift that you can only repay by giving it to someone else in turn. I learned from their generosity, and I hope I have practiced it when I could.

From that point, we sort of whirled forward until we were on an Air France plane heading to Paris. I had booked the three adults with a one-night layover in Paris and a flight on a separate carrier to Lourdes. I had a car rental waiting, but we had booked no hotel in Paris or Lourdes. I was still young enough at that point to feel no need for a fixed itinerary or certainty about my movements, even with Elie. Since Liz and I had lived in Italy, Germany and England, we both felt very comfortable with European travel and our ability to manage. I knew we could find our way to Lourdes, secure a hotel, manage meals, and take care of ourselves. We foresaw no problems we could not handle. I was less sure that we could care for Elie. I had taken special care to find adaptor plugs and a transformer that would power the feeding pump for her, but Elie brought a new level of complexity and uncertainty.

Barring some emergency, the feeding pump was the most crucial issue. Elie's nervous system was so sensitive that she was fed on a continual basis to limit the amount of food in her stomach. If she got more than one milliliter of food per minute, she would vomit. This is basically the equivalent of about four drops of baby formula per minute. She could not handle any more volume. She barely tolerated that amount, but according to the nutritionists, we had to feed her that much to ensure she did not suffer malnutrition. If we gave her too much, she would arch back, start coughing, and then suddenly projectile vomit. She was frighteningly delicate.

Her special, pre-digested formula was critical as well. During the six weeks in the hospital, we had found one formula that she could tolerate to some extent. The formula was not common, though, and we special-ordered it in multiple cases to ensure we had enough. It was not available on the shelves of any stores, and I knew we would never find it in France. One entire suitcase was dedicated to her formula. We packed enough that if we missed a flight and had to stay an extra week, we would not run out. That suitcase weighed as much as everything else we brought.

The medicines were the next problem. I wanted to have a redundant set of meds. That way, we could carry one set and pack the other in a suitcase. It was easy to imagine having a purse or shoulder bag stolen in Kennedy airport or Paris. If we lost the meds, we would have to medevac Elie out of France. I thought about special travel insurance, but I could not afford it. We were really trusting God to watch over us.

As an aside, Liz and her mother had no problem with this approach. God would take care of us. They carried their faith with a sort of fatalism that astonished me. I could trust in God to help keep things safe, but I knew He was counting on me to do the planning. Among the key mottoes in my life is the one that says, "God helps those who help themselves." The extent of Liz and Bette's faith is always hard for me to fathom. At times, it seems as if they feel they have no part to play other than riding their lifeboat on the currents that God provides. Active intervention by an individual is unnecessary. God will provide.

Beyond the feeding issues, Elie also had a terrifying habit of primitive startle seizures. They most often happened when her skin was suddenly exposed to a change in temperature. When we lifted her out of the bath, for example, she would suddenly throw her arms back and start to cry in a piteous, terrified wail as if she were being dropped. This would persist for a minute or two until we had her swaddled in a blanket again and held tightly in our arms.

At the time, we believed this was a sign of a cognitive response. She was scared because she couldn't see and suddenly her environment changed. This was her way of telling us that she was frightened. Later, much later, we learned that these probably were breakthrough seizures in a pattern of nearly continual sub-clinical seizures. In layman's terms, Elie was like an epileptic who never quite stopped having a seizure—until a year later when we found an anti-seizure medicine that controlled the condition. Even then, the medicine itself caused problems.

Elie was a remarkably fragile child then, and it is of little surprise to me in hindsight that the doctors almost unanimously gave her a very low life expectancy. So it is with wonder now, years later, when I think of us boarding a plane and blithely heading off to Europe in search of a miracle with a child who was ten days out of the hospital, only half-alive, and hanging by a thread.

※ ※

The flight was uneventful in that there were no major problems. Elie was fine on the plane, and Air France provided infant passengers with a wonderful hanging basket that swung above the seat from the overhead compartments. The feeding pump battery lasted most of the way to Paris. We spent some time on board with the steward trying to find a place to plug in the pump so that it could charge, but eventually we gave up. When the battery ran low, we took turns staying awake to pump one milliliter per minute by hand into Elie's feeding tube with a syringe.

In Paris, we secured a hotel room near Charles de Gaulle. We were staying one night, and taking an early flight to Lourdes in the morning. At the hotel, I plugged in the pump to charge, we all showered and changed into fresh clothes, and Liz napped for a bit. We decided to walk around Paris as sightseers. We had a carriage for Elie and simply continued the hand feeding as we walked while the pump charged back in the room.

We walked to the metro in mid-afternoon and rode the subway to Ile de la Cité. We visited Notre Dame first, and entered into the dark sanctuary of the church with Elie in her stroller. Inside, Liz and her mom immediately knelt down in the pews and started praying. I walked around in the back with Elie, but she began a long, high pitched cry that echoed around the quiet church. After a moment or two, a nun approached me and signaled that we needed to be quiet. I laughed since I had no control over Elie's crying, and so I left the church and waited on a bench in the small garden opposite the entrance until Liz and her mom emerged.

From there, we walked along the river to the Jardins du Luxembourg, where we had a sherbet and a drink at an outdoor café. The trees and gardens were all in bloom, and the afternoon was dry and beautifully sunny. After an hour or so, we continued our stroll along the river and crossed into the Latin Quarter where the streets wound in a maze and were filled with restaurants, small shops, and nightspots. Life almost seemed normal.

It was a beautiful July evening with the sky a darkening azure and the flowers in the window boxes all in bloom. We wandered around but spoke little. The sounds of the city life filled us with a rejuvenated sense of possibility. After being hermetically sealed in a hospital for six weeks where the only access to outside was a courtyard deep in the well of an 11-story building, the walk around Paris reminded us of life, the beautiful gift of life. We marveled at Elie, who rode in the carriage with her legs dangling over the bar and her bare feet in the breeze, and we suddenly felt lucky. Elie had survived. We had been ready to lose her, yet she was with us still and we were all walking around Paris, admiring the city and looking for a place to have dinner together.

We ate that night at a crowded Greek café with a basement room, and after dinner we took the metro back to our hotel. In the morning we were on a flight to Lourdes.

The road from the airport at Tarbes to the small city of Lourdes is dry and dusty. This southwestern part of France lies in the rain shadow of the Pyrenees, and it reminds me of southern California or Arizona. The land is green, but it feels dry and hot. The airport is small and filled with wheelchairs. The sick and their families are everywhere. Taxi drivers and many men of the region wear white shirts, slacks, and dark sunglasses. They lean against their cars and smoke, telling jokes, or they drink espresso together at the airport bar, waiting for the next plane to arrive. It feels parochial in a warm way.

There is little reason to visit Lourdes except as a pilgrim, so everyone is very used to dealing with the infirm. The thing that surprised me most about Lourdes was the warmth and hospitality of the people. I expected to find locals who were jaded, who had seen a hundred million—five million each year—sick people, and that they would be set up to prey on tourists and pilgrims. It is a cynical sense that has grown with my own travel experiences. Where many tourists congregate, the local culture becomes almost parasitic.

Lourdes was different. People were kind. Yes, of course the main road leading down to the Basilica, called the Rue de la Tour de Brie, was lined with souvenir shops. They sold rosaries, crosses, plastic images of St. Bernadette, postcards, almost any type of religious medal or icon you can imagine. In spite of it, there was no underlying current of cynicism. There were also no anti-religious shops selling joke t-shirts. The people of Lourdes make their living off of the pilgrims—that is clear—but it is a symbiotic relationship, not parasitic. Perhaps it is the shrine itself, which has a tremendous spiritual power to uplift. Perhaps it is the very moving faith of the people who visit. Perhaps it is all of these and more. Lourdes is a place that washes away cynicism. It builds strength through the power of hope.

Our taxi driver asked where we were staying. My French is very poor, but I managed to tell him that we had no place to stay and were looking for a hotel. I asked him to take us to the tourism bureau in the city. He said he could do better than that, and he took us down some side streets to a small pension owned by a cousin of his. It turned out to be very clean and perfectly reasonable, a ten-minute walk from the Basilica. Each morning, they served a lovely breakfast of croissants, fresh cream butter, and café-au-lait in a large bowl, which was included in the price. At night, they offered two sittings for dinner for a small extra charge. It was wholesome and somewhat plain—pilgrim food. It was just what we were looking for.

Lourdes is built on the rim of a bowl and its streets funnel inexorably down to a bend in the river Gave. The Basilica is located within the bend in the river on its west side. The streets within the city wind back and forth and are tightly hemmed in by old buildings that feel somewhat haphazard. The effect of these tight streets and the profusion of souvenir shops and small pensions is that you wind your way toward the Basilica without ever really seeing the church or grounds until you reach the river, and then the vision of the church and grounds opens suddenly before you. It is astonishing.

Where the Rue de la Tour de Brie crosses the river is an open bridge. The city lies to the east. The grounds of the Basilica lie to the west, and the bridge seems to form the boundary between the life of commerce and human activity on the one hand and the spiritual life on the other. Standing at the bridge, one receives for the first time the full impact of the cathedral and the sense of grandeur and peace that it instills.

Unlike many cathedrals, which are built on high spots and command a view from all around, Lourdes' Basilicas (there are two completely separate Basilicas and a handful of separate churches) are built on the lowest point, almost in a depression in the landscape near the bend in the river. This gives the main Basilica, which rests on a rock promontory above the grotto where Mary revealed herself to the young Bernadette, an unassuming grace. The grounds before the sanctuary have a 300-yard esplanade that forms an oval around a grassy verge. Trees line the oval and a statue of Mary on a plinth and column welcomes pilgrims near the bridge. To the right, the river straightens and along its edge is the Accueil de Jean-Paul II, which is a sort of hospitality center and chapel for the thousands of volunteers who come to the site to help manage Lourdes.

◆ ◆

When Liz traveled to Lourdes as a volunteer, it was early October, just before the baths close for winter, and the group stayed in the Youth Village, which is located on the grounds of the sanctuary and houses students from all over the world. The group ate meals together and stayed in dormitories. They rose at seven, had breakfast, then worked in the baths for eight hours. The baths are staffed completely by volunteers, and consist of separate men's and women's areas. Inside each, there are two granite tubs, almost like troughs, filled with the frigid spring water from the grotto where Mary appeared to Bernadette and told her to dig with her hands to find a spring that has flowed ever since and has provided many miraculous cures.

Visitors are channeled quietly and in a remarkably orderly way through the baths. They are brought into the bath room in groups of six, and they undress in privacy. The volunteers help undress the many sick and wheelchair-bound pilgrims. Each pilgrim is given a wet sheet to wrap themselves. It has been wrung out but is startlingly cold. The volunteers lead the pilgrim down steps into the bath, which is thigh deep. The volunteers and the pilgrim recite the Hail Mary in whatever language the pilgrim speaks—there is always a volunteer that speaks any major European language present—then the volunteers grip both arms of the pilgrim and help them dip back beneath the water and lift them out again. The pilgrim normally kisses a statue of Mary, and he is led back to the changing area again, he dresses and leaves the bath.

On that first trip to Lourdes, Liz and her friends worked for six days straight helping lift, dress and undress the sick, prepare them for the bath, dry them, wring out towels, help them say prayers. She says it is the most exhausting thing she has ever done, which is a lot for a woman with six children now and a pair of twin boys. She also says that after caring for Elie and specific help for a few friends with particular spiritual needs, it was the most rewarding work she has ever done.

After their shift, Liz's group would gather for the evening procession and the candlelight vigil to say the Rosary. The candlelight vigil and the Rosary procession were the two most moving things I witnessed at Lourdes. Every day at 3 pm, the thousands of pilgrims to Lourdes gather in procession to say the Rosary. The procession files in perfect order around the esplanade. The sick in wheelchairs are pushed by nuns, nurses or family members and always are first behind the priests. Groups of different nationalities follow their own priests who recite the decades of the Rosary in their native tongue. In any procession there are hundreds of different groups and languages.

And there was always perfect order. I reflect now, in hindsight, on this scene from memory and am amazed at the unity created by thousands of people speaking dozens of languages all at the same time. What distinguishes this from the prophetic story of Babel and the doomed tower? Each was intended to build a bridge to God. Perhaps it is simply a question of engineering and materials. The materials that build a bridge to God are internal—not works of the hands, but works of the soul. Perhaps it is a question of intentions. The tower builders intended to raise themselves to God. The pilgrims intended to build the bridge that allowed God to come to them.

The procession ends each evening with a candlelight vigil before the entrance to the lower Basilica. The entrance is at the center of two, curved stone walks that rise from either side of the esplanade to the piazza before the front entrance of the main Basilica. The rising ambuscades remind one of the welcoming arms of Mary. The candlelight vigil takes place in silence, enveloped within these arms, and the candles are three or four deep all the way up the ambuscades as well. The vigil, I believe, pays honor to Mary, the bringer of hope.

Such was the power of Lourdes. Joy gives strength. Back when Liz returned to Oxford and described her trip to me, I listened patiently but wondered if she wasn't captured by some kind of religious zeal. After I visited myself, I knew what she meant. Lourdes was built on a spring of hope. Hope is the basis of joy.

For Liz and her group, the end of the procession and vigil was the culmination of their work day. They walked together back to the Youth Village, ate dinner as a group, drank wine, and sat up until late evening talking with each other and telling stories. In spite of the hard work, she and the friends with her spoke about nothing but the happiness that the trip brought them. Here they were surrounded by the sick and dying, working harder than many of them have ever worked, doing things that in other circumstances would seem menial or degrading, and yet they were all happy and their mealtimes were filled with joy.

Among the many good friends Liz made was a young woman, named Gesine, and her husband, Massimiliano. They were from Rome but had a brother who was studying at Oxford. This was their third time to Lourdes as volunteers with the Oxford group. Liz sat talking to Gesine one evening. The conversation strikes me as one of the funnier experiences of our time in Oxford. It went something like this:

Liz: How long have you lived in Rome?
Gesine: I've lived there pretty much all my life. Massimiliano is from just outside Rome.
Liz: Do you have your own place?
Gesine: Right now, we're living with my parents, but we hope to move out to the country near Rome sometime.
Liz: Yeah. Living at home is a drag sometimes. I lived with my parents after college for one year while Kent and I were engaged. It was okay, but I liked being independent. We're hoping to live in the country sometime too.

The conversation goes on for a bit and is interrupted after a half-hour or so when a young South African man from the group pulls up a chair to chat. He has been on the trip before and knows Gesine.

Man: How are you doing, Gesine.
Gesine: Fine, thank you.
Man: (with a smile) Any new Caravaggios, then?
Gesine: No. Same old things.
Liz: What?

Gesine: Oh, nothing. He is teasing me because my family has some art work.

Man: Some artwork! You should see the place...

As the conversation unfolds, Liz finds out that Gesine is the daughter of one of Rome's royal families. She is a princess. An ancestor was Pope Innocent X, and her family at one time owned about 20 percent of Italy. She lives in the last privately owned palace in Rome. It takes up the whole block on the Piazza Venezia just in front of the monument called "the wedding cake." It has more than 300 rooms. They also owned, until recently, the Church of St. Agnes on the Piazza Navona in Rome. It was the family church. They owned palaces in Genoa and other cities, each of which had priceless art collections that comprised Caravaggios, Titians, Rafael, and Velazquez and sculpture by Bernini and Algardi.

She lived in one wing of the palace. Her parents lived in another wing. Liz was consoling her for having to live with her parents. We've laughed about that many times, particularly after we visited Gesine and Massimiliano in their home.

So Liz worked beside a Roman princess and her husband, who volunteered to work among the sick, taking on hard, menial labor in Lourdes. Such was the power of the place.

⊰ ⊱

We spent five days at Lourdes with Elie. It was an exhausting time because, in spite of our best efforts, we never succeeded in charging the pump's batteries. Instead, we had to hand feed Elie from a syringe, one milliliter per minute 24 hours a day. This meant that one of us had to try to stay up all night. We took turns, but often the feeder fell asleep for short periods. Many times, I would wake up with a start and realize that I had missed thirty minutes of feedings. I would give her ten milliliters to try and make up for the missed food, and Elie would wake up and vomit. It was a very difficult process.

In the morning, Bette rose early and took Elie to morning Mass so that Liz and I could sleep for an hour or two. I think this was Bette's favorite time. She rose early and wound her way down through the streets to the bridge with Elie in a stroller. The mornings were often misty by the river, and the pilgrims arriving at the lower Basilica for a dawn Mass seemed to appear out of the mists. By eight o'clock, the strong sun would have burned off the mists, and it would be a lovely warm walk back to the hotel.

When Bette returned, we ate our breakfast together. The days followed a pattern. We walked the streets a bit, found postcards, bought bread, cheese, water and fruit for the day, and then we walked down together to the grotto. When the baths opened, we stood in line. I visited the baths once, and I took Elie with me.

My visit to the baths was somewhat comical. I was tired from lack of sleep. I had Elie with me so I was very distracted because I had to hand her off to the volunteers as I undressed and prepared myself. I was worried about her having a huge startle seizure or throwing up. On top of all that, I had no real idea what to expect or what I was supposed to do. A man held Elie to the side. They dipped into the water with a hand and made the sign of the cross on her forehead. I watched her apprehensively. At the same time, it was my turn to step into the baths. I wrapped the freezing towel around me, and the cold took my breath away. I stepped out from behind the curtain and down into the granite trough. An older man held my arm from the side. I turned toward him, not knowing what I was supposed to do next. He pointed to a spot on the wall. In a little nook was a statue of Mary, about 8-inches high. He began to pray the Hail Mary. I followed him as best I could though I could barely get the words out because the cold was so startling. When I was done, he gripped one arm gently and another man took my other arm. They dipped me back into the water and I came up sputtering and trying to get my breath. I turned quickly to exit the bath, embarrassed that I was so completely clueless as to what I should do. The man took my arm and gently turned me around. He whispered with an English accent, "Some people like to make obeisance to Mary." I saw from the corner of my eye that a man in the next trough stepped forward and kissed the statue. I thought that was sort of silly, so I bowed awkwardly and crossed myself. After dressing, I emerged from the bath feeling like a stranger in a strange land.

The grotto is a small, damp crevasse on the side of a steep cliff. The rock wall overhangs the entrance and, far above, the walls of the Basilica rise out of the rock itself. The grotto extends about 30 feet into the cliff. The floor now is polished marble and an altar rests in the middle of the grotto. A statue of Mary in a sky-blue robe is set in a small alcove to the upper right side of the entrance. Moss grows on the rock walls and dampness is everywhere, but the grotto is always perfectly clean.

When Bernadette Soubirous first saw the Virgin Mary, the area was a dump for the city of Lourdes. Refuse was dropped off of the cliff and pigs were sheltered in the grottos. Bernadette was walking in the area when she felt a gust of wind and saw a small girl, dressed all in white. In later apparitions, she appeared in blue, with a blue belt, a yellow rose on each foot, and Rosary beads on her arm." In one visit, Bernadette asked Mary her name. Mary said to Bernadette, "Que soy era Immaculada Conceptiou". (I am the Immaculate Conception). For a young, poor, illiterate girl from Lourdes, the theological concept of the Immaculate Conception would have been completely alien. It was one of the things that convinced the local bishop of Bernadette's story.

According to the history, Mary appeared eighteen times to Bernadette. In the ninth apparition, Mary uncovered the spring to Bernadette. In doing this, clean water flowed in a place where only dirty water had existed. Though people at the time did not know the cause, the area had been wracked by cholera. Bernadette herself had nearly died from cholera a few years before and would be susceptible to disease throughout her life because of the early illness. The gift of pure water was a double blessing to the town. It prevented disease, and—for some of those that bathed in it or drank from it—it offered miraculous cures. Crutches hang on the wall, a memento of the cures that pilgrims have received.

By the last visitations, Bernadette was accompanied by tens of thousands of people from all over the district. Mary asked Bernadette to request that the people build a chapel and that they pray in penance. The Lourdes Basilicas are the result.

❦ ❧

On the fourth day, Liz and I rented a car and drove to Vielle-Aure to attend Anthony and Laurence's wedding. It was the first time that we had left Elie since her mini-stroke in our living room in Cedarville. Bette planned to spend the whole day in the Basilica or on the grounds. She would walk Elie up the path in the forest behind the church and visit the Stations of the Cross. I think Bette was glad to see us go for a while.

It was a beautiful, sunny, warm day with no clouds. We picked up the car and drove out of Lourdes toward the highway at Tarbes with the windows open and the wind flying in the car. Liz wore a pretty black dress. I wore a dark suit. It was the first time in four months that we felt like we were doing anything normal, like we were living again.

I suspect that we probably looked like ghosts. We had not been in the sun for months. Our complexions were wan and stretched. We wore the constant worry and concern of Elie's illness and the care of her slow and troublesome convalescence in our faces. Liz was thinner than she had ever been. I was just plain tired.

And yet, for those few hours in the small village near the Pyrenees, surrounded by friends, filled with the joyousness of a wedding, we were very happy. We laughed. We danced. We drank a little wine. The guests sang songs from their native countries during dinner. The French booming out a chorus to a regional song. The English doing their best at God Save the Queen. The few Americans (Liz, me and one other couple) making a lame attempt at Oh Susanna. We drove back to Lourdes laughing and holding hands.

It was a short escape but, like Lourdes itself, it was a taste of happiness and company and it filled our exhausted and depleted spirits. It reminded us of the goodness, the beauty, the value of life.

CHAPTER 15
The Velveteen Child

Once upon a time there was a couple who lived very happily in their small home in the woods. They went for long walks together, skated on the frozen lake at midnight in the early winter, cooked meals and drank wine with friends. They were very happy.

They had a little baby. She was adorable, and they loved her very much. At night, when they had put her to sleep, they took pictures of her and sent them to her new grandparents. They played with her on the floor during the day, took her skating (wrapped inside her daddy's coat to protect her from the bitter winter winds), and sang to her in the evenings as she bounced in her chair.

Late at night, as they lay in bed with the baby sleeping in her bassinet beside them, they would ask each other in whispers if this was real. Life was so good. Could it be real?

The little girl was very happy too. Her parents doted on her, showed her off at church, visited with their friends who had children. She had plenty to eat. She giggled and loved to bounce, when she was not bothered by gas pains or teething. And she grew quickly into a winsome baby girl, not quite an infant anymore.

But one day she grew sick. Her parents had to leave their home and take her to a new place. She tried to laugh, but her mouth did not work right. She could not lift her hand. She was quieter, and her parents were too.

They moved into a hospital. The little girl's parents wanted to try and fix her so that she was all right. She would do whatever they wanted. They cried a lot at night, but they tried to hide it from her. Still, when it was very dark and the little girl was nursing by her mother's side, she could feel her mother's short breaths and feel the bed shake when her father sobbed. She heard them ask sometimes in whispers late at night, "Is this real. Can this really be happening to us?"

The little girl knew it was up to her to help her mommy and daddy, and while they put her to bed at night, she heard them asking God please not to take her away. She listened to that and she thought, "Well that's easy. When God asks me to go with him, I'll just say no and tell him that I'm going to stay with my mommy and daddy instead."

Soon the doctors came, and then some nurses, and they took the little girl into a room where she fell asleep.

And when she woke up, a beautiful woman named Mary was standing next to her. The little girl waved hello because Mary seemed almost like her mommy. She was surrounded by light, and the light seemed to sing to her.

Mary asked her, "Do you want to come with me, my child. We're going to see our Father."

The little girl thought about it for a long time. It was a hard question because she knew that Mary's Father was good and her heart told her to go, she knew she would be happy with Mary and that eventually her mommy and daddy would be happy too, but then she remembered her mommy's prayers late at night and her daddy crying. She remembered her promise and how easy she thought it would be.

The little girl told Mary that she was going to stay with her mommy and daddy for now, but that she hoped Mary would come see her sometimes too.

Mary kissed her on the forehead and told the little girl to call for her when she was ready to go. Mary would come whenever she called, and until she called Mary would send angels to keep her company.

The little girl fell back asleep and slept for a long time. When she awoke, her real mommy was rocking her gently and singing a lullaby. She was very glad to be back. Her daddy was sitting in a chair nearby. They were still in the hospital.

The little girl's mommy touched her forehead where she now had a long scar. It stretched from beside her ear to the middle of her scalp. She had bandages on her head, and blood seeped from a tube. Underneath, her hair had been shaved away. Tubes were stuck into her arms and down her throat. Her wrists and ankles had stitches from where the doctor had cut her to put other tubes.

"We have loved you so much that we've done this to you," said her daddy. "We've worn you to pieces."

Her mommy kissed her on the cheek and held her very tight. "I'm glad you're still with us, little girl. We love you so much."

The little girl listened to them for a while. She was glad to be back. But when the angels came, she wondered if it was real. Was she really with her mommy and daddy or was she with the angels. They floated around and above her, they sang to her, they showed her pictures of Mary and her baby.

The little girl wondered if she was still with her mommy and daddy, but whenever she remembered her promise, she would hear her mommy's voice calling her: "Elizabeth. Elizabeth. I'm here little girl. Come back to me," and the little girl would feel her mommy again.

Time passed. Sometimes the angels came and sometimes they stayed away for a long time. The little girl waited patiently for them. She listened to her mommy. She let her daddy kiss her and rock her each night.

And sometimes, late at night, she heard Mary's voice whisper very softly, "Just call me whenever you want. We are waiting for you." Mary was not there, just her voice. But it comforted the little girl.

"Not now," she answered. "My mommy and daddy still need me. Not quite yet."

And she knew that both her parents and Mary were real. She knew them both, without knowing how she knew, knew they were both right there, all the time beside her, watching over her.

∼ ∂

After returning from Lourdes, I left alone for Michigan. Returning to a cold, empty house, one thousand miles from my wife and daughter was one of the bleakest moments in my life. I needed to be there to work, maintain income, ensure health benefits, and prepare the house if there was some remote possibility that Liz and Elie would return to Michigan.

The doctors had expressed doubt that Elie would live more than six months to a year. Moreover, she needed therapy and access to the doctors on a regular basis. I had very little hope that I would have my family back with me in Michigan. I wondered if I would see Elie again or if she would die before I could even visit.

Prior to Elie's first diagnosis, we had been in the Upper Peninsula for eighteen months. We had made some new friends, but none were particularly close at that point. I remember sitting in my living room in the dark and quiet and wondering how I could possibly stand to remain there alone.

A few days after I returned, the parish priest, Father Mike, visited me and we had lunch together. Mike was a young priest, extraordinarily gentle, and a talented musician. Later, the friendship between Mike and both Liz and I grew very strong and has remained so despite years and miles. That afternoon he was a brother to me.

We sat at the small table in our kitchen. The house itself was a shambles. I had torn out most of the walls in the kitchen, dining room and entry hallway and was in the process of redoing our interior when Elie suddenly lost the use of her arm. We left for the hospital without looking back. I'm not even sure I locked the door. I was now returning seven weeks later.

There have been moments in the chaos and jumble of our young family that I have cried out intemperately for a little time to myself with no family to bother me. Back in Michigan, I had it, but I never wanted it less. Going to work was a chore. I had clung desperately to some meaningful work when I was in New York City; now I had trouble concentrating on anything in a sustained way.

At the same time, work on the house in the evenings seemed pointless. It was a form of busywork to keep my hands occupied and my mind empty. I found myself staring out at the lake for long periods, not really thinking about anything, just staring. With Elie and Liz so far away, the separation from what really mattered was enervating, and I felt lost. Even when I was able to accomplish something in the evenings, it still left me feeling overwhelmed. I had no kitchen, the bathroom was gutted, the ceiling in the living room was bare studs, and the list of tasks I needed to accomplish to make any progress stretched out beyond what I could reasonably see finishing myself.

Father Mike pulled into my driveway one Saturday afternoon. I was building a stud wall by the back door. I don't think I had showered in a couple of days, nor combed my hair much at all. I looked slightly wild and very tired. At nights I had been working until 1 am because I dreaded the quiet of my house and hoped each night to fall straight to sleep when I switched out the light. I rose at six and worked on the house for an hour before heading to my office.

Father Mike drove his MG, a sporty green convertible that he kept in immaculate condition. Father was the parish priest for four churches across two counties and sixty miles in the eastern Upper Peninsula. The furthest church was on an island and required a ferry ride to get there. He said Mass in each of them on the weekend as well as visiting with his far flung flock in the days between. He put a lot of miles on his cars, he was always working, and he was always nonplussed. He was a priest who loved his vocation.

I saw him pull up the driveway and climb out of his small car. Although we had attended Mass together each week and Liz was a devout parishioner, Mike knew I was not Catholic. I looked out the back window and wondered why he was coming to visit me. I admit that I dreaded at some level the questions from anyone about how I felt, and the need to explain what we knew about Elie's condition. I thought briefly about not answering the door.

Father entered the hall and said hello. "Kent, you're always working on something," he said.

He was a trim man, about five foot nine. He had a very well-kept beard that was grizzled but full. Looking into his twinkling eyes, he was like a young Santa Claus if only he gained twenty or thirty pounds and his beard grew longer and more silver. He had long fingernails on one hand for playing his guitar, a staple of his Mass, and he wore his priest's collar and a clean black shirt. He moved with a contained self-assurance as if his backbone were formed of sprung steel, and you had the feeling that it gave him a resilience to adversity, as if he could take a heavy blow from fate and spring right back to where he was. Father Mike was a man that you could not dislike.

"Plenty to do around here, Father," I said, waving at the chaos of deconstruction.

I invited him in and put the kettle on for tea.

Before he became a priest, Father Mike worked in an airplane factory in Wisconsin, and work with his hands was never far from his mind. He seemed to take real pleasure in things made. Whenever he visited after I had made a piece of furniture, he always wanted to scrutinize it very carefully to see how it was built, to notice the joinery and the careful polish of the wood.

He walked around my construction efforts and I showed him what we planned. He listened and nodded at everything. "It sounds great, Kent. I'm sure Liz will really like it," he said.

I made two sandwiches and we sat down.

"How is Liz holding up?" he asked.

His first direct question surprised me. I expected a question about Elie. Almost everyone else wanted to know about Elie, hear about the surgery, the brain tumor, the result. It felt most often as if people were simply probing for news, for information they could share with other people. They seemed to ask solely to be able to tilt their head, furrow their brow, and shake their head sympathetically. I am generally a private person, and questions about Elie cut so deeply into me that I dreaded the interviews of well-meaning friends.

To me there was so much unanswered. How was Elie? We didn't really know. How could I say she was? Would she ever talk? Would she walk? I didn't know, but if I voiced those concerns, people didn't really want to go that deep. They wanted a quick soundbite, and don't make the news too bad, please. Keep it short, with a tough beginning, a little mystery, and end with something upbeat.

But that wasn't how I really felt. I didn't know if there was an upbeat ending. I faced a destructive and paralyzing sense of the unknown, but that was something nobody wanted to hear from me.

Father Mike was always different. He did not want news. In fact, he has always been one of the few people I know who did not desire the commerce of gossip. He wanted to know about Liz, and by extension he was asking about our relationship and me. It was as if Elie's condition was of secondary importance because there was nothing he could do about it—except pray, and that he was doing anyway—but the emotional and spiritual well being of his friends was something he could help. Talking to me directly and with Liz by phone was something he could do, and in so doing he could help. Father Mike was a true minister and shepherd.

I found that his disarming first question, obliquely touching on rather than assaulting the things that were most important to me, made me suddenly want to tell him everything. I had spoken with many friends before Father Mike visited, but I had never said much. They didn't really want to hear the story—they only wanted the surface. Father was very different.

Over the next two hours, I told him everything that we had gone through, what we hoped, what we feared, what we expected. He listened to everything and said almost nothing himself. I told him that I felt overwhelmed at needing to be in Michigan in order to maintain an income and health insurance when my only child was likely to die in New York. I told him that I was manically trying to fix our house so that it was habitable for Liz and Elie, but that I didn't ever really expect them to come back to live here. I told him that I worked until one in the morning to wear myself out so that I couldn't think enough to contemplate that I might not ever see my daughter again. I told him that I didn't understand what I was supposed to do, that I didn't understand what was happening to me, that I had trouble avoiding despair.

And Father really only said one thing that I remember. He said, "Yours is a beautiful sacrifice. I will keep you in my prayers, as will most people in this community and people in many other places as well. Pray yourself. God will help you."

And when he left late that afternoon, I wondered two things. First, what advice had he given me with any practical value? And second, why did I feel so much better?

I attended church the next morning, mostly out of a feeling of solidarity with Liz, whom I knew would be at St. Peter's in Port Washington with her family. I stood in the back, still undressed and unwashed. I didn't really want to be seen. I left before the end of Communion to avoid having to speak to anyone. I drove home and started to work on the bathroom.

The middle of the next week, a man pulled into my driveway late one afternoon. He drove a sky blue pickup truck with no tailgate and dents in almost all of the panels. The front fender was held on with heavy gauge wire. The bed was piled with junk—old Rebar, a toolbox, a pair of boots, huge pipe wrenches.

He unwound himself from the cab, and when he stretched out to full length was over 6 foot 3, rangy and bow-legged. He wore a filthy baseball cap and a greasy Carhart jacket. His mustache was full and dark, and his eyes seemed black. His hat said, "Dunn Hill Iron Works." He looked a little like an outlaw, and I was not sure why he was in my driveway.

He walked around the back of the truck and lifted out the heavy toolbox. Then, he walked up the driveway and knocked on the back door. He introduced himself as Randy Dunn, the local blacksmith. He stepped inside the back door. I offered to put on a pot of tea. He said no, he didn't have time, and that he preferred to get right to work.

I must have looked completely perplexed. I had not asked for any help, and I knew that I could not afford to pay anyone. I could barely afford the materials for the house. I said nothing, but simply watched as he poked around, looking over what I had done.

He turned to me and, seeing my puzzled look, smiled and said, "We heard about your daughter. There are a lot of people praying for her. I came to see if I could help you out at all."

Over the course of the afternoon and early evening, he helped me plan the construction and get the framing for the bathroom roughed in. Randy was a jack-of-all-trades—a master electrician, a plumber, a blacksmith. He had worked in construction, fishing, timber. I later found out he was a prodigal son who had once driven his car off the dock in town and into the bay in one particularly wild night, but that he was now an elder in the United Congregationalist church in town. He had me smiling all afternoon with his stories and observations. For a few hours of his companionship, I forgot my sadness.

Toward late evening, we sat on the steps by my backdoor. In a quiet moment he said, "It ain't easy to know why this stuff happens. I trust Jesus, though. He's in charge." He paused. "We're all praying for you," he said again, and left as quietly as he had come.

I was perplexed after he left. Was his visit a sort of missionary work—like the advertisements from the Mormon Church that urge us to do good deeds for our neighbors? How did he know I needed help? I went to bed earlier that night after calling to tell Liz about my new friend. I pondered what he had done more than what he had said, but I wondered about that too.

Randy returned the next afternoon on his own, and helped me get the bathtub set and the Wonderboard screwed in so I could set tile.

The next day, three of Randy's friends showed up at about 5 pm. They carried tool belts and dinner, for themselves and me, which their wives had made. They spent the evening putting up drywall in the entryway, telling stories about each other, and keeping me company, while I tiled the bathroom.

On Friday, my dad surprised me when he pulled into the driveway. In the back of his rental car, he had work clothes and a tool belt. He was taking a few weeks off, he said, to help me fix the house so that Liz could live in it when she and Elie were ready to come home.

CHAPTER 16
Faith, Hope, and Charity

I laugh to write it now, but as I sit in the kitchen this morning, I am expecting my sixth child in two months. He will be named Avery after Avery Cardinal Dulles. I have twin boys who turn five in May. A little girl named Hannah who turns three in one month. Alex is six and already a first grader.

Elie will be ten years old this fall.

What began as musings over a wrenching twist in our life path has become something of a life work. Both this account and Elie herself. Nine years ago, Liz and I sat for hours in our small living room in Michigan, rocking Elie and talking to her to keep her from throwing up. And when she did vomit, we fought to ensure she didn't aspirate and get pneumonia. The doctors said she might live to 18 months.

Yesterday evening, after I had put the other children to bed, I walked downstairs to Elie's room. Liz sat with Elie on her lap, wrapped in a blanket, not quite rocking because of her condition, but holding Elie, comforting her. And as Liz arose to make her way to bed, I took Elie up and sat with her for 45 minutes, talking to her, trying to warm her up with my body heat, keeping her tightly wrapped in a soft velour blanket, a nightcap on my lap.

So much has changed. And yet, so little has changed. I still come down each evening to hold Elie. We still try to keep her warm by wrapping her in blankets and laying a hot water bottle on her legs. She still lies abed, having never regained any power to speak, walk, talk, take care of herself or even smile. She is still my little pumpkin.

Yet Elie has somehow exceeded all expectations. She has changed our lives in ways we never could have imagined.

∽ ∾

We have had nannies and au pairs helping us along the way. Our favorite was a girl from the Czech Republic, who stayed with us for a year. Her name was Lucie Mayerova, and she was one of the nicest people I have ever known. She helped Liz and me watch the kids and keep the house functioning. She made everything by hand. She loved walking in the woods.

At one point, her mother made gifts for our three boys. They always have been fascinated by knights and all that goes with them—swords, jousting, whacking each other over the head with random blunt instruments. They are healthy boys and, over the past year or so I have realized part of my life mission is to ensure that they make it to 21 without killing themselves or each other. Lucie had told her mother about the boys' love for knights, so her mother sewed and sent a set of three cassocks—one green, one blue, and one red—that might be worn by a knight's squire. On the front of each she had sewn a golden shield, and on the front of each shield a symbol. One was a cross, the second was an anchor, the third was a heart.

These are the symbols of faith, hope and charity.

Liz had told me these were the three most important virtues—the supernatural virtues—but I began to wonder. What makes these the three greatest virtues? Why hope more than, say, courage? And, more importantly, what does it mean to live by these virtues? What do they really mean in the composition of a good life? And, lastly, how do I relate these to Elie? What is the meaning of her life in contemplation of these three virtues?

Faith

This is perhaps the most difficult for me because it is the most complicated. Faith is the belief in God and of His presence in my life. But what of that presence?

I have faith that God is the Creator of all life. I further have faith that he is present in my life—present in the many, subtle whisperings of my soul that happen throughout each day. God is not just the Creator, but God is creation. The word "inspire" is derived from the same word as spirit, spiritus, to breathe. Those thoughts, those sudden realizations, those creative impulses, those nagging understandings that guide me to decisions or action—all are inspired in me. They are not as clear as revelations, not as if a window were opened and I could suddenly see clearly. These inspirations are more a whisper on the wind, easily dismissed until you grow accustomed to listening for them. These whispers do not come from me. They come to me.

This, I imagine, is the Holy Spirit. The dove that descends to Jesus in the river is a visual manifestation of the hand that guides. Yet the Holy Spirit is not, in my imagination, so much the dove itself as the cooings of the dove—subtle, barely audible except in the crepuscular moments of our consciousness and not at all unless you are listening for it. The spirit as a sort of voice, heard at quiet, contemplative moments, or at moments when it is not expected. And, like a dream when we awake, it is easy to ignore or to push toward the recesses of our consciousness, there to be forgotten. Only as we acknowledge its presence do we even really hear it. Once we believe it is God working within us, it becomes much more difficult to ignore.

This is the root of my faith. God—a direct God—who inspires and guides me directly. God and the divine spirit.

Yet Liz often reminds me that the fundamental belief in Christianity revolves around a trinity. Pater, Filius, Spiritus Sanctus. Filius. The Son.

Christ is a problematic figure for me. Do I believe he lived? Yes. Do I believe he was God become a man? I don't know. Do I feel a compelling urge to know? No.

If I accept that Christ lived, then the fundamental question that answers whether he was God become a man is the Resurrection. If you believe in the Resurrection, that God raised Christ from the dead in fulfillment of all of His prophecies and that Christ walked around as a visible spirit, visiting his friends and relatives after the Crucifixion, then everything else Christ says must be true.

Christ says, "I am the way, the truth, and the light. Nobody comes to the Father but through me."

So, if I believe in the resurrection of Christ, then I must believe what he says. But what does this saying mean to me, who believes in a direct and active God the father? Is Christ saying that nobody finds God except by believing in God as man, or nobody finds God except by believing in God, period? Christ is God. The Trinity is like separate folds in a single blanket. So if we believe Christ is God speaking, then the interpretation is open.

This is one of the fundamental truths about faith. God never seems to make faith simple. It always requires first that one admit they don't know, they don't control, they don't understand. "I don't know why, but I believe," is the first step toward knowing, yet God always leaves room for doubt, for the actions of a free will. He is even open to wordplay at times, as evidenced by his lovely interchange with Peter, whose name, "petra" means "rock" in Greek. The Gospels, I think, show a profound sense of humor when Christ asks the disciples, "Who am I?"

Peter answers, "You are the Messiah. The Son of God."

Touching Peter, Christ says, "Upon this rock, I found my church."

The simplest reading is that Christ is signifying the faith—or the leap of faith—which Peter makes in his statement. The faith exemplified by Peter's sudden candor is to be the basis of Christianity. Christ appears to be saying: Believe that I am God and you shall find God.

At the same time, there is a clear reading in which this is Jesus identifying the leader of his apostolate after his death and resurrection. A part of the Catholic reading is that in this sentence, Peter is named as the first head of the Church. Peter becomes the first father of the church, the first Pope.

"Upon this rock." Does he mean that Peter is the rock? Peter is petra in Greek. Does he mean that Peter's faith in Christ as God is the rock?

Christ's playfulness even in the contemplation of his Passion is unavoidable. If the latter is true, Christ names Peter's faith as the foundation of his Church even with the foreknowledge that Peter will renounce him. I can almost see Christ's tongue in his cheek as he says, "Upon this rock, I found my church." Peter's spontaneous belief, unpremeditated in any way, is the rock of faith. Yet that rock proves fragile, and Christ knows it. Within a very short period, Peter contradicts his faith when he denies Christ three times and says, "I do not know this man." In the confusion of Christ's sentencing and crucifixion, Peter has a sudden crisis of faith, perhaps because of sudden doubts about Christ's Godhood, perhaps out of a more personal fear for himself in the face of a riotous mob.

Is Peter himself the foundation stone of the church or does he express in a sudden inspiration the rock upon which faith is based—the "leap" in a leap-of-faith. I tend toward the latter. Although Peter proves inconstant in the immediacy of Christ's crucifixion, it is his sudden, spontaneous belief—almost as if a child were answering—straight from the heart, inspired by the spirit, which underlies the faith Christ describes as fundamental to salvation. Though Peter denies Jesus in the immediacy and confusion of the crucifixion, perhaps that doubt only serves to strengthen Peter's conviction after the Resurrection. Peter's acknowledgement of Christ's divinity is the acorn that Jesus knows will grow into a mighty oak.

So can I make that same inspired statement? Do I believe that Christ was God? If I do so, I do it absent the inspiration of Peter. The cooing of the dove provides little guidance here.

Is it important to me? I am less sure of this answer. Perhaps it is, but I feel no compelling urge to know. The Holy Spirit, that divine messenger to the inner ear, compels me in many ways, but about this it remains silent.

Perhaps God is testing me. I will give you guidance in many areas, but this leap of faith I will not bridge. Enter this as a child.

Perhaps the question is not critical. Perhaps Christ as messenger was simply saying that no one comes to God but through knowing God, and the paths to that are at least as numerous as three.

And Elie's role? Has she built my faith?

She has certainly drawn me closer to God and strengthened my belief. To the direct God. But has she brought me closer to Christ? Hard to say. Hard to say.

Hope

This is a trait so important to the human condition that I almost place it higher than faith. Without hope, we are left with despair, what Kierkegaard called the "sickness unto death." With hope, our lives, no matter how bleak, are bearable in some measure.

Yet the very root of hope is faith. A belief in a higher power, a greater meaning, a hand guiding us toward heaven. The concept of heaven itself is the ethereal expression of hope.

Beyond faith, what are the ingredients of hope. Certainly humor. Probably courage. Definitely imagination. These all are tools that God has given us to persevere in life, to maintain our hope. Even in our very darkest moments, we retain faith in a divine plan, courage to proceed through our hour of darkness and uncertainty, we imagine the alternatives, a better life, an end to the difficulties, and we retain, at crucial moments or soon after, the ability to laugh at our own condition. In this way, we have hope. Faith, in a sense, becomes a means to hope.

Indeed, the idea that God has given us a toolbox is very compelling. The tools are the virtues: faith, hope, charity, justice, prudence, fortitude, and temperance. Add to these, humor, imagination, and strong red wine, and we enter armed into a world in which we can either choose to act on behalf of goodness or on behalf of evil. Evil is not something that God inflicts upon us. Evil is the result of choices made by individuals with the free will God has given us. Use God's toolbox and you will make choices on behalf of goodness. Make your decisions based upon the sins—pride, envy, gluttony, lust, anger, greed, and sloth—and your decisions will act against goodness.

Mahatma Gandhi had a modernized list of the evils perilous to humanity. They are:

> *Wealth without Work*
> *Pleasure without Conscience*
> *Science without Humanity*
> *Knowledge without Character*
> *Politics without Principle*
> *Commerce without Morality*
> *Worship without Sacrifice*

One could argue, for example, that pleasure without conscience is gluttony. Gandhi's is a list of evils that arise from decisions based on the deadly sins. The choices made by free-willed people based on the sins will lead to evil. Gandhi's list does not alter the virtues.

We are given the power to choose good. God acts through us when we act with virtue.

Charity

Love. Charity is love.

When tested by the Pharisees, Christ said that the most important commandment was to love God with all one's heart and all one's soul. And the second most important was to love thy neighbor as thyself.

Love is the most important virtue, and the absence of love is despair. In this way, too, love is inextricable from hope.

This is the most difficult virtue to explain in Elie. She evidences a pure, uncontested love. In some ways, she returns love. I know it clearly and Liz knows it too, but it is almost like faith—we know it because we believe it.

But receiving love from Elie is not at issue. The issue is giving love to Elie. She absorbs it, all of it. Without ever giving a sign of surfeit, she takes all the love that everyone can give her.

More than the handmaiden, Elie herself is the hand of God, the dove that descends. A child, purely innocent and utterly dependent, is the gateway to divinity. Elie has been a centering point for God in our family.

CHAPTER 17
False Expectations

I characterize the time after Elie's surgery as long periods of ignorance and optimism punctuated by intense disappointment and dashed hopes.

The doctors left us with no clear sense of Elie's future. They spoke a lot about the plasticity of a child's brain and how intense therapy might help to reprogram her to gain some normal functions. The nurses echoed this optimism. The social worker helped us set up the therapy schedule in Liz's hometown. They all expressed optimism, and we soaked it up. Without it and Lourdes, we probably could not have left the hospital; the challenges would have been too daunting.

After I left for Michigan, Elie began a heavy regimen of physical and occupational therapy. Liz packed her in the car with the feeding pump and all of her other requirements two times a day and drove to the physical therapy offices. There, Elie stood on a stander to strengthen her legs and skeleton, rolled on a ball, played with head-activated switches, ranged her muscles and stretched, and on and on.

I saw little of this, but instead experienced it through the telephone. Liz described to me each evening what Elie had done that day. How Elie had pressed the switch with her cheek. How it showed progress.

The tank of optimism was full and it continued to fuel us for these weeks.

Liz also told me by phone about other problems she was facing. Elie cried all the time. I had experienced it to some extent in Lourdes, but it seemed to get worse. Elie had gas from her feeding regimen, which caused cramps. The pediatrician thought that Elie's digestive tract was not accustomed to the formula. Each time we thought we found a formula that worked, a week later we found it caused as many or more problems. We switched her feeding countless times, accumulating cases of formula in Liz's basement that we would end up not using.

At the same time, Liz began a regimen of working Elie's legs like a bicycle. It helped Elie pass the gas more easily, and provided her some limited relief. I would call at 8 pm and have Liz tell me that she had done the bicycle for three hours that afternoon, trying to stop Elie's crying. I remember one call where I spoke to Liz's brother, Frank, who was home from college and had spent the last two hours in the late evening doing the bicycle with Elie because Liz was worn out and had gone to bed.

It was distant to me. Liz explained what they were doing, but I did not see Elie's discomfort or hear her non-stop crying, so the description of the heroic work Liz and her family were doing held less impact. Liz was often tired but almost always cheerful, so I never really understood how difficult this all was. And because I had no idea what Liz was going through, we made no effort to get additional help until I returned and saw for myself.

The summer continued in Michigan. Thanks in part to my new friends and largely to my dad, we finished the bathroom, reconstructed the kitchen with hand-built cabinets, laid a new floor, installed a wood-stove for heat, replaced the windows in the bedrooms, and put a roof on half the house. There was plenty of work to be done yet, but after eight weeks of nearly non-stop work into the late-night hours, it was a home that Liz and Elie could potentially live in.

I began to think about bringing them back to Michigan.

Liz had regular follow-up visits with the pediatrician that had seen Elie at NYU. She was assessing Elie's progress, or lack of it. Toward late August, she wanted to schedule a follow-up MRI and a meeting with a doctor named Jeff Allen with the pediatric oncology department at NYU. It is possible that she was sharing information about Elie all along with us and we weren't hearing it, but I think instead that the pediatrician was guarded in what she told us. We were filled with optimism. Each evening Liz told me about progress that Elie had made—how she sighed when she was picked up, how she had gripped the switch in therapy, how the therapist would compliment Elie on her great range and low muscle tone. It all seemed very positive.

The pediatrician underlined this optimism to some extent by referring again to the plasticity of the child's brain and how therapy could show significant benefits. Elie might be able to re-learn certain skills.

In hindsight, we were clearly blinded by our hope and optimism. Of course, no one really knew Elie's potential with absolute certainty, but the NYU doctors—Wisoff, the pediatrician, Jeff Allen—probably had a strong sense of Elie's future. Our optimism must have disarmed them in a way and made it very difficult to speak directly about disappointment. I have come to find that the very best doctors are the ones that admit and act on the knowledge that they really don't know what makes us tick. They are all acting on probabilities, and those probabilities are informed by their experience and the experience of other doctors. The most experienced doctors, however, know that there are always exceptions and surprises. The best doctors are open to possibilities, and in that sense ours were waiting to see.

So we carried along with a high sense of hope until our meeting with Jeff Allen.

The stated purpose was to see the progress of Elie's tumor and whether additional treatment—chemo or radiation—made sense. We were extremely nervous because the tumor, as Wisoff and Epstein had described it, was benign but had grown as if it were a malignant tumor, fast and invasive. The surgery had removed 90 percent of it or so, but it still felt like a time bomb for us. Beyond that, we had heard enough horror stories from our time on the cancer floor of metastasis and new tumors appearing after surgery, and we had seen enough parents crushed by broken hopes. We feared bad news and the chance we might have to go through all of this again. Our concerns clearly focused on the tumor. How big was it? Was it growing? Were there any new tumors? Should we treat it?

I flew back from Michigan to join the meeting. I arrived a day early and saw, over one afternoon, what taking care of Elie involved. I immediately decided that we needed to find nursing help for Liz. It was so clear coming in from the outside that, in hindsight, I do not know how I had not realized it before. Probably it was mostly Liz's cheerfulness. She never complained to me, so I had no idea how difficult the care was. I called the social worker who had helped with our discharge from NYU and we scheduled a visit by a nurse to explore setting up regular in-home nursing care for Elie.

The nurse came in the evening. He was a forty-five year old man, very nice, with graying hair and glasses. He spent twenty minutes with Elie, then an hour with us answering questions. He would do some checking into our insurance and other options, but he felt it was very likely that we could at least get help during the nights. The relief in Liz's tired face was clear. She was worn out.

The other thing that he told us had to do with Elie's gas cramps. He suggested that her feeding tube may be a part of the problem and that we could "vent" her through the tube. Nobody had ever explained this to us. We needed an attachment for the "mickey," which is the port into her stomach, but with it we could open the vent and release any gas. I was astonished and grateful to him. Two months of nearly constant discomfort for Elie and mind-numbing work for Liz might be solved by something as simple as a small piece of plastic tube we had not been told about. I began to wonder what else we had not been told about.

The nurse left saying that he would call us the following day and that they would begin immediately looking for nurses for the night shift. He hoped they would have someone to help us within a few days. True to his word, Liz had nursing during the nights by the end of the week. Though she slept near Elie even with the nurse there, Liz actually began to sleep at night.

We drove Elie into the city for the meeting with Dr. Allen. Bette and Frank came, as did Liz's sister Kristin, who is Elie's Godmother. Liz and I dressed Elie in a special dress for the occasion. We talked nervously the night before about what we would do if the tumor had grown, how we hoped not to put Elie through chemo or radiation, how we would care for her no matter what and would never institutionalize her. For me, it was a huge blessing just to be back with my wife and daughter. Living in Michigan had been lonely and far too distant.

The pediatric oncology office is a sort of sad and funny circus. In the waiting room, kids are going in every direction, just as normal kids would. They are crying, or laughing, or playing with each other on the floor. The only difference is that many of them are hooked up to intravenous poles that administer the chemical treatments, and that they wheel these behind them as they play. The other difference is the parents, who all show in their faces that they are collateral damage in a cancer war.

We sat for fifteen minutes in the waiting room. Nobody said much. Bette held rosaries in her hand and counted the beads off quietly as she prayed. Liz and I held hands. Elie had been to an MRI center near her house two days before. We brought the scans with us and handed them to the receptionist when we arrived. I had tried looking at them the night before but they meant nothing. We all felt this was a critical meeting that would, in a sense, unfold to us Elie's fate. The tumor could be growing, she might need treatment, she might not be a candidate for treatment, she might have had a miracle and there would be no tumor. Our future seemed to lie in the reading of those scans.

As she often did, Liz dealt with her tension by talking to other people. Within ten minutes, Liz and her father were talking to a young, teenaged girl named Patricia, who sat in a chair beside them. The girl had found out she had a brain tumor when she was eleven. It was advanced and malignant, but her surgery had been very successful and she went into remission. She had chemo and radiation. She described how hard it had been to find out that the tumor had begun growing again. She was on her third round of chemo. I sensed in listening that her development may have been affected by the tumor or the treatment, or both. Yet her composure was magnificent. This child sat on her own. She was resigned to her fate, even accepting of it. Instead of turning in on herself, she turned outward. A week later, we got a letter from her. She told us how beautiful she thought Elie was and how sad she had been to learn about Elie's tumor. She said she was praying for Elie every night and she asked us to pray for her.

One of the things Bette constantly said during these early months of Elie's surgery and follow-up was, "God gives you the graces you need when you need them." This means that if you ask, God will grant what you need to overcome your hardship. It does not mean that

God will necessarily grant what you pray for, but rather what you need. We prayed all the time for a miraculous cure for Elie, but at this point, it had not been God's will. Yet we still had Elie. She was not taken from us when all the doctors said she would be. We were given fortitude and courage when we needed it. We were able to accept when we needed. We were strengthened in our marriage rather than torn apart as so many couples with terminally ill children are. These were God's graces.

Patricia had them as well. In fact, she was so filled with grace that we were all immediately drawn to her. Composure, fortitude, empathy, love. These were her qualities, and they shone from her. When someone asks the question, "Why does God create brain tumors?" I now think of Patricia, and Elie, and my friend Mike Coda at work, who eventually died of his brain tumor yet who endured his illness with so much grace and humor. The answer is: to make us more beautiful, more like Him, to fill us with grace. It is a great paradox and mystery that suffering is the path to holiness. Those who ask the question about God creating brain tumors focus on the imperfection of the body, yet they should focus on the perfection of the soul. God is not revealed in what happens to us but in how we react to what happens to us. Goodness is revealed—or not revealed—in the choices we make and the intentions that drive those choices.

∽ ∾

After about thirty minutes we were brought into a conference room with a long table. We seated ourselves along one side of it. A few minutes later, two young residents entered, followed closely by Dr. Allen. He pushed the MRI scans up into the light boards on the wall, then turned around and seated himself. He smiled. "Well. How is everybody?" he asked.

"We're fine," I said, trying to read his expressions.

"Nervous," Liz said at the same time.

He proceeded to work through the scans, pointing to various pictures as he spoke. Elie's tumor had grown back some, but it was not significant. It was still clearly there in the middle of her brain. It would probably affect things like temperature control, hormone production—meaning she may never grow or develop normally. Eventually, he said, it would grow and potentially affect areas like breathing or other critical functions. He paused, then added: The stroke, of course, is the more serious issue immediately.

We all sat and listened to him, not really understanding what he was saying. None of this was very new, so it did not catch us off guard. What he said next, however, did.

Liz asked if he was recommending chemo or radiation to treat the tumor since it was growing back. He paused for a moment more, looked at both Liz and me, then dove in.

"No," he said.

"Why not?" I asked.

"There is little reason to treat the tumor further. First," he said, "she may have trouble handling treatment. She is so compromised already that surviving chemo is questionable. Second, the tumor is only one problem. The stroke is another, and there is nothing we can do about that. Third, there is the whole question of quality of life..." His answer trailed off.

I asked, "Why do you keep mentioning the stroke. I thought we were here to find out about the tumor."

"Look," said Dr. Allen. "The tumor isn't what has made Elie the way she is. It's the stroke that has caused so much damage to cognitive functions. We can treat a tumor. The stroke is untreatable. The damage is permanent."

Nobody said anything. I think we were all trying to compute what he was actually telling us. I asked, "What about the rehabilitation and therapy? You all have said that a young brain can redevelop new pathways and learn things in new ways. Isn't that possible?"

He waved us back over to the light boards. "Look at these scans here," he said, pointing to a series in the middle of one sheet. "All of this dark area is just fluid. There is no brain left here at all. Major parts of her brain are gone. The parts that are left are centered around the back, the medulla, core functional areas for breathing and other involuntary body activity. But, in terms of redeveloping new pathways to restore anything approaching a normal development, there's nothing left for that."

"What are you saying about Elie's future?" Liz asked.

"Well, it's always hard to say," Dr. Allen told us. "I don't have a crystal ball and I've been wrong, but I would expect her to remain this way for the rest of her life. She is in a persistent vegetative state."

Persistent vegetative state.

That was the first time we ever heard the term. We had heard people called "vegetables" before. Someone in a coma or brain dead. This, I supposed, was the medical term for the same thing.

"Are you saying she will never get any better?" Frank asked.

"Yes," Dr. Allen said. "I think this is permanent and she will regain little, if any, function."

There was complete silence as we sat in the room, trying to comprehend this new twist.

For two months, we had been living on hope, working toward Elie's rehabilitation. The chance of improvement was a light at the end of the tunnel. We didn't know what she could regain, but we had always thought it would be something. Dr. Allen pulled a curtain down on that hope—so abruptly, in fact, that we did not believe him and continued to deny it for some time after the meeting.

He was right to do so. False expectations leave an ugly stain. But the suddenness with which this hit us left us speechless.

"How can you say 'vegetative,'" Liz asked at last. "She reacts to us. She sighs when we pick her up. She cries when she has gas or pain. She startles and cries when we take her out of the bath. She's definitely improved since she was in the hospital."

Dr. Allen continued to talk in the empty space. He ameliorated around the edges. Nothing was completely certain. He cannot predict. Only God knows. But this is his trained opinion. Kristin was wiping tears from her eyes. Liz was stunned and she continually kissed Elie, whom she held on her lap. Frank and Bette sat quietly.

I felt as if I had checked out of the conversation. Finally, I regained enough composure to ask something. It was the first thing that came to my mind. "How long will she live?"

Dr. Allen almost seemed to welcome a change of topic. "That's impossible to say," he told us. "As I said, I don't have a crystal ball. But, in my experience of 30 years, a child like this will have complications only partially related to the tumor or the brain. Most often they get pneumonia because they are already so compromised. Or, they grow but their brain can't really cope with the demands of growth. Eventually they just run out of capacity to support their body."

"How long do you think?" I asked.

He looked square at me. "Could be six months. Could be thirty years. It depends on the care that she gets." He looked back to Liz. "Most of the kids like this don't live much past eight or so."

◈ ◈

The car ride home was quiet. We talked about what Dr. Allen had said and what it meant. Frank still focused on the tumor and still worried if Elie would ever be able to see. Liz focused on the fact that Elie could live until she was thirty. Bette focused on the unknown and how everything was in God's hands. Kristin supported Liz and tried to take an optimistic view. The women all fussed with Elie, kissed her, patted her cheeks.

I sat in the back staring out the window and thought back to our meeting in Dr. Wisoff's office. I had told them then my worst fear, which had been for my child to end up totally disabled—a vegetable. Now it had come true. I had been worried about ending up with a child who—in my own words to Dr. Wisoff and Epstein—"was a vegetable or on life-support."

Persistent vegetative state.

The words kept ringing in my ears. Elie would never get any better. My worst fear had been realized.

I thought back to the time before Elie was sick that I had stood in front of my living room window and stared out at the lake, saying in a silent prayer, "God, I believe in the Father. If Christ is important to my life, then show me some kind of sign."

Was this a sign? It seemed more like a cruel practical joke. I had asked for a sign, and God had given me a task of realizing my greatest fear and living with it. My first child, dying and yet not dying. Neither dead nor, in a sense, really alive. Six months. Eight years. Thirty years. No clear vision of the future. No clear sense of what would be expected of me, of us.

I thought about another one of my early prayers. When I first met Liz and was considering asking for her hand in marriage, I remember that I prayed only that my life would never become commonplace or dull. I prayed that it would contain mountains and valleys and that I would never wish to erase those in order to create stability. I prayed that I would never become bored with life.

I thought about the contradictions in my prayers. How I asked for valleys once, but when I hit one of my life's biggest valleys, I prayed for a quick easy way out of it—for, in essence, more stability and less fluctuation.

There is an old French saying: If you want to make God laugh, tell him your plans.

I had not heard that at the time, and I probably would not have appreciated it. Now, though, I laugh to think of God watching over us like an actual father. Just as I sit in a kitchen chair in the dark and watch my twin boys in the next room, unbeknownst to them, as they plan quietly how to get an extra cookie from Mommy after dinner, and I laugh.

So must God watch over us, all children in his eyes, planning our lives without a clear sense of the big picture. Sometimes God must chuckle—with a loving tenderness—but He must chuckle.

CHAPTER 18
Private Thoughts

This is a moment for which I have prepared hundreds of times, which I have rehearsed, which I have spoken to myself over ten years and in many different ways. I have delivered my daughter's eulogy hundreds of times. I have imagined her gone as much as I have realized she is still here.

This daydream comes upon me unexpectedly; imagination is uncontrollable. I find myself thinking about Elie, or living without Elie, mostly when I am alone. I have lived many times what it will be like never again to kiss her cheek or smell her sweet skin, to bury my face in her neck, to stroke her hair as she lies on my lap.

I have spoken this eulogy in cars, in the woods, in a boat. I have spoken it mainly when I was alone, out loud with the tears streaming down my face. But I have also prepared it in my head at a party or as I sat with a crowd of friends at dinner, my thoughts drifting far beyond the conversation until I have had to stop my train of thought because I knew that within moments I would choke up and start crying and nobody would have any idea why.

I have delivered the words with love, with pathos, with anger. I have looked for hope. I have spoken of despair.

God has, at various times, been a merciful God who gave me my child for longer than He had originally planned. At others, I have complained about God snatching away my first child's promise.

I have spoken words like these so many times that it should come easily. But it doesn't. It has never come easily—how could it. I have always realized the finality of this moment. That is when my heart begins to tear. The desolation of finality follows. Her death is final. It is monstrous. And it is desolate.

I've often laughed that Elie had three goals in life. One was to remain my little baby girl forever. One was to avoid the pain of teething. And the last was never to be put down, to be held by someone continuously through life.

She has done quite well except for the teeth. She has always been our little baby. Even when we had a baby who was smaller by far, Elie was the baby.

It amazes me that so many people have touched her, held her, rocked her. So much family. Dozens of the most caring nurses we could hope for. Many priests have held her and all have prayed for her continuously since her illness. She has been comforted and loved by more people in her few short years than many of us in a lifetime. And being held, being touched, has been her way of touching others in turn. We touched her physically. She touched us spiritually.

We hold in greatest honor those who have cared for her on a daily basis. Let their names spoken offer them the honor and gratitude they deserve.

Bob and Donna Smith
Laurie Lewis
Jean Steiner
Marilyn Miraglia
Dr. David Ragonesi and Dr. Gregory Liptak, *(whom we recognize with particular distinction for their compassion and commitment)*
Linda Gavigan
Linda Foster
Robin Miechkowski

Beth Ygeal
Jill Bevel
June Douglas
Carrie Barry
Dr. Bernd Holler
Mary Pat Hutchins
Sue Potoczak
Margaret Burrows
Father Michael Steber
Jane Havranek
Lisa Goff
Barb Vera

Perry Cooper *Raynell Hart*
Theresa Kimball *Linda Morotini*
Donna Gretz *Theresa Palmeri*
Chris Davis *Debby Noyes*
Christine Kennedy *Tammy Simmozin*
Mary Hopkins
Father William Delaney

Her greatest caregiver, of course, I hold in greatest honor. Her mother, Liz, who single-handedly kept Elie with us for 10 years purely through a devoted mother's love and fierce tenacity.

And we release her.

Of her death, what good can be said: It was short and merciful. It only lasted ten years.

Of her life, what good can be said: I feel I could write a book about it, and yet it is like the whisper of wind on a single blade in the tall grass.

I cannot point to many things that I have done which were wholly good, but caring for Elie is one. She was a burden, yes, but she was also a gift.

And it is my great hope that if I ever make it to heaven and stand before God, I will be greeted there by a little girl with blond hair and a sweet smile who welcomes me and introduces me to God. And God will laugh and say, "Don't worry. It wasn't ever really as close a call as you thought. Anyone who cared for Elie got a free pass."

Goodbye my beautiful girl. God's speed.

∽ ⌒

That is what I would say, at least today, if Elie were to die.

CHAPTER 19
John Paul

In 1997, Liz and I decided it was time to take a vacation. Elie was almost four and we had never left her side since the surgery. We were up most nights, one of us rocking her, comforting her, trying to put her back to sleep after she vomited.

Liz had had two miscarriages after Elie's surgery, both of which were devastating emotionally, and then we finally conceived and gave birth to a wonderful, quiet, blond and curly-headed little boy named Alexander. He was almost a year old when we began to consider a trip. I told Liz that I wanted to take her back to Italy for two weeks when Alex stopped nursing.

Liz has a very high inertia hurdle, and it took nearly four months to convince her we could do it. We planned with Liz's parents about leaving Elie and Alex with them. We searched for and found a nursing service that would take care of Elie at Bette's house. Liz's sister offered to be there as well to support Bette. I talked about what we might do on the trip, and Liz began to think about a visit to Rome. Almost none of this convinced Liz we could leave our children behind. Liz felt it was too much of a burden on her mom. Then she felt it was self-indulgent for us. Then she worried about how young Alex was and whether it would permanently scar his psyche to be left for two weeks at that age.

In the end, three things convinced Liz we could do it. First, she began a series of correspondence with the Vatican about the possibility of attending a Mass with Pope John Paul II. Second, our friends offered us the use of their apartment in the city of Modena while we were there. Third, her mom in particular convinced Liz that fourteen days away from the constant worry of Elie while knowing she was in the best of hands as well as time away from the tension of a nurse always in the middle of our family and our very small house would be good for our relationship. These three things, plus the sheer exhaustion Liz felt, finally convinced her to go.

The Vatican correspondence began from a conversation Liz had with her mom, who knew that some people—on very rare occasions—had a private audience with the Pope and sometimes attended his early-morning prayers and Mass. Liz would have been quite happy, I think, with attending a general audience in St. Peter's square—which we ended up doing—but the thought of a private meeting with John Paul really motivated her.

First, Liz asked our family friend, Father Delaney, to write to the Bishop requesting his help in securing a private audience with the Pope. Liz wrote a letter accompanying Father Delaney's request in which she described Elie and our strong desire to ask the Pope personally for his prayers for Elie.

The secretary for the bishop wrote back a few weeks later and said, in part:

> *As regards the special privilege of participating in the Holy Father's morning Mass, we have just recently received guidelines from The Vatican, via the NCCB,*

> *informing us that the great number of such requests renders most impossible of fulfillment. Thus Bishop McGann regrets that no petition will be presented to accommodate Mr. and Mrs. Gilges's wish.*

Liz was completely undaunted. She decided to bypass an uncooperative Bishop and write a letter to the Secretary of State for The Vatican instead. She addressed her letter simply to the Secretary of State, The Vatican, Rome. Like the first, this letter was carefully handwritten with a description of Elie's illness, our desire to ask the Pope's personal blessing, and a picture of Elie.

To my great surprise, a month later Liz received a letter from Monsignor J. Harvey, Assessor for the Secretariat of State at The Vatican. He said:

> *Dear Mrs. Gilges,*
>
> *I am writing in reply to the letter which you addressed to Monsignor Stanislaw Dziwisz.*
>
> *The sentiments which prompted you to write are appreciated, but I regret to inform you that it is not possible for His Holiness to comply with all the many requests to attend the Mass celebrated in his own Chapel. You may wish to contact the Prefecture of the Papal Household, which is the office in charge of Audiences and other papal ceremonies. The address is as follows…*

At this point, we were one month from departure. I was working hard on details for the trip—flights to NYC to drop the kids with Bette and Frank, further flights to Zurich, a car in Zurich to drive south, nursing shifts for Elie, food and medical supplies, a doctor in New York in case of emergencies. I gave little thought to the likelihood of seeing the Pope and, since our trip was basically without itinerary—we were going to go where we liked and find places to stay when we found a town or pension that looked interesting—I was not even convinced we would make it all the way to Rome anyway since we had the apartment to use in Modena and what we really needed was a lot of rest and no set plans.

It would have been completely natural to give up on the idea of meeting the Pope with the receipt of this last letter. Instead, Liz wrote yet another as directed by Monsignor Harvey, this time to the Prefecture of the Papal Household. Given the shortness of time before departure and the month that it took previously for a reply, in this letter Liz asked for a response at the address of our friends in Rome, Gesine and Massimiliano. She figured when (I thought "if") we got to Rome, we would have the response waiting for us.

We left with little expectation other than that we would try to drive to Rome if we were feeling up to it. For my part, I forgot all about the letters, to which I had paid very little attention. I figured we could visit St. Peter's and maybe participate in one of the Pope's outdoor Masses if we were lucky.

❦ ❦

In the Gospel of Mark, there is a particular passage that I have thought about ever since Elie was diagnosed. It is the story of Jairus.

> *When Jesus had again crossed over by boat to the other side of the lake, a large crowd gathered around him while he was by the lake. Then one of the synagogue rulers, named Jairus, came there. Seeing Jesus, he fell at his feet and pleaded earnestly with him, "My little daughter is dying. Please come and put your hands on her so that she will be healed and live." So Jesus went with him.*
>
> *A large crowd followed and pressed around him. And a woman was there who had been subject to bleeding for twelve years. She had suffered a great deal under the care of many doctors and had spent all she had, yet instead of getting better she grew worse. When she heard about*

Jesus, she came up behind him in the crowd and touched his cloak, because she thought, "If I just touch his clothes, I will be healed." Immediately her bleeding stopped and she felt in her body that she was freed from her suffering.

At once Jesus realized that power had gone out from him. He turned around in the crowd and asked, "Who touched my clothes?"

"You see the people crowding against you," his disciples answered, "and yet you can ask, 'Who touched me?' "

But Jesus kept looking around to see who had done it. Then the woman, knowing what had happened to her, came and fell at his feet and, trembling with fear, told him the whole truth. He said to her, "Daughter, your faith has healed you. Go in peace and be freed from your suffering."

While Jesus was still speaking, some men came from the house of Jairus, the synagogue ruler. "Your daughter is dead," they said. "Why bother the teacher any more?"

Ignoring what they said, Jesus told the synagogue ruler, "Don't be afraid; just believe."

He did not let anyone follow him except Peter, James and John, the brother of James. When they came to the home of the synagogue ruler, Jesus saw a commotion, with people crying and wailing loudly. He went in and said to them, "Why all this commotion and wailing? The child is not dead but asleep." But they laughed at him.

After he put them all out, he took the child's father and mother and the disciples who were with him, and went in where the child was. He took her by the hand and said to her, "Talitha koum!" (which means, "Little girl, I say to you, get up!"). Immediately the girl stood up and walked around (she was twelve years old). At this they were completely astonished.

> *He gave strict orders not to let anyone know about this, and told them to give her something to eat.*

※ ※

In my chair by the window in Michigan, I asked for a sign to know if Jesus was important in my life. Elie was struck with a terminal illness. Now I was Jairus.

When we flew to Lourdes just after the surgery, I thought about the possibility of a miracle. I think it is natural to project oneself into a situation like this. I often wondered if Elie's illness was a message from God to me or, even, if it were a test of my faith. Perhaps, I sometimes thought, if I could just believe—if I could believe without doubts that Elie could be cured—perhaps there was hope for a miracle. When I bathed in the holy waters at Lourdes with Elie, I thought, "Please, God, grant us a miracle like Jairus and so many others who have come to Lourdes for help." I thought it was possible that God could cure Elie, but I didn't know whether to believe that He would.

Jesus went to Jairus' house to raise the dead child because Jairus had the faith to ask for Jesus' help and the certainty that Jesus could cure his daughter. Jesus commanded, "Don't be afraid; just believe."

The other part of this passage that has always struck me is the faith of the bleeding woman. She knows if she can just touch His robe, she will be healed. She does not have to speak to Jesus. She doesn't need to draw attention to herself. She only needs to touch His cloth, and she knows she will be healed. She knows Jesus is God. It is a step beyond faith. She doesn't hope to be healed. She knows.

When we returned from Lourdes without a miracle cure, I wondered if a miracle might have happened if I could have believed more fully. If I could have stepped beyond belief and known. What if Jesus were walking through the grotto curing people and I were there:

would I have had the courage and faith to approach Him with Elie in my arms and ask Him to save her?

I wonder if faith with Jesus physically present would be easier. If we see a miracle happen, then we know it is possible for Him to cure us. But if we see only the relic crutches from bygone years hung from the wall of the grotto, is it more difficult to believe? To know that God would cure us if we are not afraid and just believed? Faith removed by 2000 years, at first blush, seems more difficult.

Yet what was it like for those people in the desert of Judea 2000 years ago? I imagine they were inundated with prophets, faith-healers, and mountebanks. There were probably many who tried to claim the title of "teacher," or holy man. Jesus was different, but how obvious was that difference before the fame of his miracles began to spread. I imagine the towns he visited being places where "news" spread from doorstep to doorstep, where rumor and gossip were the media for transmitting stories about Jesus' miracles, where people developed a skepticism about the next "holy man" who made claims of great powers of healing. Moreover, Jesus again and again asked after he performed miracles that the subjects not talk about what he had done. If they acceded to his requests, first-hand accounts were even rarer.

All of this is by way of saying that it might seem easier for us today to have believed if we were in the presence of Jesus, but even the Apostles sometimes had trouble believing—and they lived intimately with Jesus and saw many of his miracles. In the story of the storm on the lake, the Apostles wake Jesus from sleeping and, after calming the storm, Jesus asks them, "Why are you so afraid? Do you still have no faith?"

Again and again, Jesus questions the faith of those closest to Him. He asks the disciples, "Who do people say I am?" and they answer that people believe he is John the Baptist, or Elijah, or one of the prophets. Even for those who lived with Him, who saw Him, who witnessed the miracles He performed, it was not easy. Everyone knew Jesus was a very holy man. He clearly had an aura of holiness and wisdom. The people called Him "teacher" or "rabbi."

Although I paid little attention as Liz wrote her letters to The Vatican, still I began to daydream about what I would do if we were to meet Pope John Paul II. To me, a non-Catholic, John Paul was the holiest man I knew. He so clearly radiated goodness, conviction, positivism, courage, faith. All of the virtues were displayed in him; his holiness was palpable. I thought with a thrill when I daydreamed about meeting him that he was the closest person to Christ on earth. His holiness bespoke a closeness with God. I would call him "teacher" for his wisdom and goodness. Is that any different from what people thought about Christ in his time?

In these daydreams, I imagined myself dropping to my knees in front of him, holding Elie out in my arms, and begging him to touch Elie so that she might be healed—because I knew that if Pope John Paul II asked it of God, God would grant his prayer. I knew it. All I had to do was ask.

And yet as I considered the unlikely possibility of meeting the Pope, I grew afraid to tempt it. Maybe God wanted Elie as she was. Maybe her purpose was not to live a full life, but to touch people through her illness. What if I asked John Paul to save Elie and he lifted me up from the floor and said he would not ask that of God? What if? What if? I might actually get a chance to ask God, through Pope John Paul II, for a miracle, but what if it didn't happen. For whatever reason. What if God did not grant us a miracle? Then what of my belief?

It was up to me, I thought. If I believed enough, I would try.

We departed in early October for New York with Elie and Alexander in our arms. We left the children with Liz's parents, things went smoothly, and in less than 18 hours we were in the Zurich airport together, renting a car from Hertz and loading our duffles into the back. Both of us were jet-lagged and tired, particularly Liz who had been up most of the night before our flight getting a new nurse oriented.

We decided to start south through Switzerland and find a place to stay on the way. One of the great pleasures I always found in Germany, Austria, and Switzerland was that no matter how remote a place you found, up steep, tortuous single-track roads into the most rural parts of the mountains, at the top there was almost always a small Gasthof or pension. It is usually part of a farm, run as a way to create additional income, and it is almost always clean, cheerful, and has hearty meals available.

I drove through the lakes district of Switzerland. Liz slept with her seat reclined all the way back, though I tried to wake her a number of times when the scenery was too amazing for me to let her sleep anymore. She was so soundly asleep, however, that she lifted her head for a few seconds and said how nice it was without even opening her eyes. Then she dropped back down into a sound sleep.

About two hours from Zurich, I decided I needed a rest and that before we left the mountains, I really wanted Liz to see them. I pulled off the highway into a small town, found a dingy little Gasthof near the train station, and had a cup of tea. The town already lay in shadows within the valley, but the sky was clear blue above us and the sun was bright on the mountain sides. I wanted to get us up into the sun.

When we finished, I found a small, single lane road heading steeply up one side of the valley. A tiny sign at the edge of the town indicated a small farming village up the mountain (it turned out to have three houses, one of which let one room for the night), so we followed the road up five miles of windy switchbacks until we reached the mini-community halfway up the mountain. A quick check inside with the owner of the pension and we had an airy, wood-clad, upper-level room for the night with skylights and windows that looked out across steep grass fields toward the valley and the jagged Alps that surrounded us. We were the only guests. The bed was covered in the white down comforter so typical of the region, and when we opened the windows, the sun and warm fall breeze flowed in with the sound of tinkling cow bells from across the hillside.

We undressed, made love, and then fell into a deep sleep under the comforter until early evening, when the breeze in the window grew cold. The next day we set out on a long walk across a mountain path, ending finally at another Gasthof where I had a wheat beer, Liz had her favorite Orangina softdrink, and we sat on the porch in the sun and wrote postcards home to Elie and Alex.

Our trip progressed with methodical indolence. We spent a night above the shore of Lago Maggiore and ate dinner at a small tavern that we found walking in the hills. We had a fantastic lunch at a trattoria in Trento en route. Eventually we made our way to Modena and our friend's apartment, which is just outside of the old city. There we spent four or five days exploring the city and the region around it. One day we went hiking in the Apennines and climbed a wonderful mountain but stopped short of the top when we reached a knife-edged ridge that was about four feet wide and well-worn but gusty with a sheer drop. We decided together that we had come far enough and that the sunny fields below us were good recompense for giving up reaching the top.

Another day, we stayed in Modena and had lunch at a tiny café hidden in a courtyard behind a delicatessen. Our friends' business associate, who had let us into their apartment and given us other directions, made the reservation for us. We showed up at the appointed time in the deli, gave our names at the cash register and were ushered—in great secrecy it seemed to us—behind the counter and to a small room in the back that looked out onto an alleyway and brick wall with a cellar door opposite ours. There were three small, square tables and a very round, sweating, and good-humored man who seated us, brought a first glass of wine and proceeded to laugh and make small talk while he changed from his deli apron to a smart looking sport jacket.

Liz and I both speak marginal but passable Italian, so we understood the basic gist of his jokes and description of the menu and wines. Essentially, lunch was decided for us and with each course, he trotted across the alley and down the steps into what was, as we soon found out, a vast wine cellar, returning a few minutes later with a wine accompaniment. Two other tables soon filled, one with an attractive Italian couple—Liz and I idled away that afternoon trying to decide if they were married or lovers—and the other with a group from California, including two artists, one of landscapes and the other abstract. It was a most enjoyable afternoon!

The other outing that was particularly memorable was to Verona.

Verona is one of my absolute favorite cities. It's a northern Italian city with all the charm of Italy but that kisses up so close to the foothills of the mountains that one almost feels oneself further north. It has a beautiful river that circles the old city with lovely stone bridges, and it is ringed by hills at the further limit with a stone wall encircling. It feels like a city fortress, safe, clean, almost Germanic in its ways, but with a warmth and character that are distinctly Italian.

Before this trip I had two very fond memories of Verona. The first is from a visit there when I was in college. I stayed in a hostel and walked all over the hills and through the surrounding country. I also went to the opera.

The center of the city is dominated by a massive Roman amphitheater, and during the summer, Verona stages open air opera in repertoire. I saw Verdi's Aida and Fanciulla del West by Puccini. They were fantastical affairs with horses and elephants on the stage during the opera, and gelato and wine venders wandering along the upper, stone seats during intermission, calling out their wares to the listeners. The Italians, in fine spirits, would stand up here and there during intermission and re-sing arias from the previous act under a twilight sky—each competing with the other for the applause of the crowd. It was pure fun.

The thing that stuck in my memory from that time in Verona, however, was a particular restaurant. I was on one of my walks and ended at the old governor's mansion, which was a square brick building atop one of the hills outside the city center. In front was a large stone piazza and at the end of that was a massive brick wall and balustrade that looked down on the city. I sat up there reading for a long time, and when I grew tired I decided to explore by walking down the steep steps in the center of the wall that led in the general direction of the city center.

One flight of steps down was a landing with a little walkway leading along the middle of the wall. I followed it and at the end I found, through a gate and down another short flight of steps, the most marvelous looking porch at the front of a restaurant which was built into the wall and recessed back into the hillside. Huge plate glass windows faced onto the city. I stood just above it at mid-day, looking down on the umbrellas that shaded elegant tables on the porch, and I thought wistfully that some day I would like to bring a girl there for dinner.

But since I had no money and no girlfriend at that point, I tucked the thought away and wandered off toward the city to find a bakery and cheese shop for my dinner.

The second memory of Verona was during the period when I was courting Liz and she was studying in Florence. We traveled north together and stopped in Verona sometime in early-December. We got beds in the girls and boys dormitories at the same hostel I had stayed in before, and we walked the old city.

The city was much quieter. The productions of summer were done. All of the German tourists were gone. Verona had settled back into a quaint, provincial town. We walked the main road just at dusk and snow began to fall. It was the large, fast-falling snow that quickly turned everything white and covered people's hair and shoulders. As we walked, we stumbled onto a small Christmas market in the middle of the old city. Liz and I had very little money, but Christmas was coming so we spent the evening buying small gifts for her to take back to her family in a couple of weeks. I was staying behind for Christmas as I had little money for a flight home and was still trying to make a living as a freelance writer. I thought about Liz leaving, and I realized I wanted to be with her always.

∽ ∾

The fourth and final night we spent in the Modena apartment, I told Liz to dress nicely for dinner because I had a surprise. At about 6 pm, we set out from Modena in the car. Two hours later, we entered the outskirts of Verona. After stopping a couple of times to consult my map, I steered us onto a narrow road lined with Lombardy poplars that wound up a fairly steep hill toward a square brick mansion.

At the top of the hill, I parked in a small lot behind the building and with a great air of secrecy, I walked her out onto the piazza toward the wall that looked down over the city. The night sky was going dark and the lights of Verona spread out below us.

Liz laughed. "This is very romantic," she said. "It's a long way to come for a romantic view, but it's romantic. I love Italy."

We stood there for a few moments. We kissed. "Are you hungry," I asked.

"Are we having a picnic up here," she asked. "I'm a little overdressed for a picnic and I'm kind of cold."

I put my forefinger to my lips and guided her over to the wall and steps that led down.

"Kent, where are you taking me?" she asked. "These heels aren't made for brick stairs all the way down to the city."

"Just trust me," I said.

Liz followed me down the steps. We wandered along the walkway and at the gate, I paused then asked her to look over the railing—we had arrived for dinner.

The plate glass windows were warmly lit. The porch was lit by candles. The umbrellas were spread out and our table on the porch was set with fine silver, a glass decanter of chilled wine, and candles.

"How did you ever find this?" she asked.

"I'll tell you over dinner," I said, and led the way down the steps.

That night we arrived back at the apartment very late. Liz had slept in the car, but I was exhausted and dropped heavily onto the bed and immediately into a deep sleep. An hour later, I half woke to the sound of Liz giggling and I was vaguely aware that she was kneeling on the bed. She giggled again.

Without saying a word, I knew why she was giggling.

"You're pregnant, aren't you," I said sleepily. She giggled again. "Uh-huh," she said. "I just took the test. It's two weeks today. Look."

I rolled over. She held the plastic test kit in one hand. Sure enough, it had a clear blue line across the little window. I laughed.

"You're a maniac," I said. "Let me go back to sleep. I'm exhausted." Then I mumbled, "I love you," and dropped off into a deep, contented sleep.

≈ ≈

After four days in northern Italy, Liz began to talk about going to Rome. I was not all that supportive, just because it seemed like it imposed structure (and a very long drive) on what to this point had been beautifully spontaneous. Liz really pushed, though, so we left Modena and drove south toward Tuscany.

There we found a hotel on the outskirts of Siena. We parked the car in their garage, and spent the day wandering in the city. We also bought return bus tickets to Rome and, in the evening, called our friends to see if we could visit with them. They, very graciously, offered again to let us stay with them, and we accepted.

Just as Liz was about to hang up, Gesine mentioned that there was a letter addressed to us from the Vatican. Liz had Gesine read it to her, then said goodbye. She looked up at me, beaming.

"Kent," she said, "they've asked us to write a letter to the personal secretary of Pope John Paul and to drop it at the bronze doors when we arrive in Rome."

Our time in Rome went quickly. Gesine's parents welcomed us to a family dinner, served at noon, in the living quarters of the palace. Gesine's father is the Duke of Norwich and her mother is an Italian noble. We spent about half of our time with Gesine and Massimiliano, visiting out of the way restaurants and seeing views of Rome that few get to see. The other half, we spent at St. Peter's or in various waiting rooms, trying to get tickets to the Wednesday Mass held in St. Peter's square.

One afternoon, we walked with Gesine to Piazza Navona and up to the door of a very grand church called St. Agnes. Gesine pulled out a set of keys and opened the door for us to slip in. I asked how she managed that, and she explained that the church had belonged to her mother until the 1980s, when she had given it to the Church. Gesine talked about having come to play in the church when she was a child and how her family, like all of the noble families in Rome, had only recently given up the right to name a Bishop to the church.

After a long wait and a series of trips to different places, we managed to get tickets to the Wednesday general audience. Liz and I showed up at St. Peter's square an hour early. It was already filling fast with people. We found seats about halfway back in the square next to a young couple from New Jersey and along the main aisle that Pope John Paul II would travel in his car to the stage. In talking, we found out that we both had hoped to see John Paul close up, and we laughed that this was the personal audience we had wished for—us and 20,000 other people.

After Mass, we requested tickets to visit the crypts beneath St. Peter's, and we were told to return at 4 pm. We then went out for lunch and walked around the Palatine hill. We had been in Rome four days, and we planned to head north again the following day. It had been a wonderful visit, but our trip was growing to a close and we wanted to visit a close friend in Germany before leaving Europe.

At about 3 pm, we returned to St. Peter's. I sat outside and read. Liz made another visit to the church. We met up just before 4 pm in front of the door to the crypts and were ushered down with a small tour group into the vaults beneath St. Peter's church. This was one of those parts of the trip in which I had very little interest but Liz really wanted to do. In the end, Liz had trouble dragging me out of the crypts because I found it so fascinating, and we ended up dropping back from our tour group and joining the next English speaking one to hear more.

Most interesting to me was the fact that the pinnacle of the dome of St. Peter's rises directly above the original altar of the church Constantine founded. A glass enclosed excavation shows you the original altar stone, which is buried beneath the current floor of St.

Peter's. More interesting still is that directly beneath the altar is a single stone crypt, and when opened in the 1960s, this crypt was found to contain bones from a single, male human—all of the bones except for the feet! Scholars believe this is the tomb of St. Peter himself, and the feet are missing because the common practice in the Roman Empire for taking down a body that had been crucified upside down was to chop the feet off at the ankles and let the body drop.

Of course, nobody knows for sure whether it is St. Peter in the crypt, but I found the history fascinating. It also made me really begin to think about Peter, the Apostle.

One of the parts of the Gospels that I have always found most touching for its glimpse of our human foibles is Peter's betrayal of Jesus.[7]

> *Then Jesus told them, "This very night you will all fall away on account of me, for it is written: "'I will strike the shepherd, and the sheep of the flock will be scattered.' But after I have risen, I will go ahead of you into Galilee."*
>
> *Peter replied, "Even if all fall away on account of you, I never will."*
>
> *"Simon, Simon, Satan has asked to sift you as wheat. But I have prayed for you, Simon, that your faith may not fail. **And when you have turned back, strengthen your brothers.**"*
>
> *But he replied, "Lord, I am ready to go with you to prison and to death."*
>
> *Jesus answered, "I tell you, Peter, before the rooster crows today, you will deny three times that you know me."*

---

[7] I have pulled together passages from both Mathew and Luke to give a single account of Peter's betrayal. The emphasis is my own.

> But Peter declared, "Even if I have to die with you, I will never disown you." And all the other disciples said the same...
>
> ...Those who had arrested Jesus took him to Caiaphas, the high priest, where the teachers of the law and the elders had assembled. But Peter followed him at a distance, right up to the courtyard of the high priest. He entered and sat down with the guards to see the outcome.
>
> A servant girl saw him seated there in the firelight. She looked closely at him and said, "This man was with him."
>
> But he denied it. "Woman, I don't know him," he said.
>
> A little later someone else saw him and said, "You also are one of them."
>
> "Man, I am not!" Peter replied.
>
> About an hour later another asserted, "Certainly this fellow was with him, for he is a Galilean."
>
> Peter replied, "Man, I don't know what you're talking about!"
>
> Just as he was speaking, the rooster crowed. **The Lord turned and looked straight at Peter.** Then Peter remembered the word the Lord had spoken to him: "Before the rooster crows today, you will disown me three times." And he went outside and wept bitterly.

Simon Peter, who had shared life so closely with Jesus, had seen the miracles of the dead raised and the lame cured, had eaten and slept with God those many months, even Peter could not hold faith when Jesus was taken away and beaten. If any human being in history should have been able to keep faith, it should have been Peter—Jesus' best friend. Yet Jesus knew Peter's weakness because, in the end, it is our human weakness. When truly tested, even Peter's faith could not hold.

And yet the beauty that I find in this passage is what comes after. Imagine Peter's shame at being told he would betray his best friend—betray God—and then finding that he did exactly as he was told he would do. Imagine the shame from being pierced by Jesus' gaze across the room as He is being whipped and beaten, the shame of denying your best friend—let alone the one whom Peter himself declared to be the Christ. Peter leaves the tribunal and weeps. But God has foreseen more than just the betrayal. He has already said to Peter, "And when you have turned back, strengthen your brothers."

Peter's failure is the very core of human weakness—a failure of faith at the moment we need it most. Yet Peter's story continues, and in that story is the foundation of human strength. I imagine Peter spending the rest of his life remembering the shame of his betrayal of Jesus. I further imagine him living every moment henceforth trying to redeem himself for that failure, an effort that ultimately leads to his own crucifixion, upside down on a hill above Rome because he felt he was not worthy to die the same death as Jesus. Before dying as a martyr, Peter spent roughly 30 years teaching and leading the growth of Christianity.

Faith comes not from our nature but from our trial and failures and our desire to be redeemed. Resurrection is the heart of Christ's Godhead. Redemption is the heart of our humanity.

※ ※

Liz and I returned from the crypts to Gesine and Massimiliano's apartment in the palace at about 7 pm. Since it was to be our last night, we had planned to go out together for a simple meal. Gesine had a nanny to sit for her two children, and the four of us walked out into the evening streets of Rome for dinner.

After dusk, we returned to the apartment. The nanny gave an account of the children to Gesine and, just as she was putting on her coat, mentioned that we had received a phone call just after we had left for the evening.

Liz and I looked puzzled. "Nobody from home knows we're here," Liz said to Gesine as Gesine translated the nanny's rapid Italian.

Gesine smiled at us. "She says it was the Vatican, and they have asked you to be at the bronze doors at 6 am."

Liz and I just stared at her. "That's all they said," I asked. "Nothing else?"

Gesine fired off a question to the nanny, who was rather impatient to leave herself. "That's it," Gesine said. "Be at the bronze doors at 6 am. They did not leave a return number or name but they asked if you would be bringing the child."

Liz turned to me. "Kent, I think we are going to Mass with the Pope."

We spent the next two hours getting ready for the morning. Gesine and Massimiliano were very kind to let us stay with them for an extra night. They went even further as to call up to Gesine's mother to ask what was appropriate attire for a papal audience (it was common custom for a new Pope to greet the noble families in Rome, so Gesine's mother had been to at least three papal audiences).

Appropriate attire for a woman was a black veil or scarf, and since we had none, Gesine's mother dropped hers down into the courtyard from their apartment on the other side of the palace. She laughed on the phone when Gesine asked if she could help us, "I'll have to go digging around for my Pope box and it will take a little while. It has been so long since I needed to use it last as this Pope has been around for ages."

We pressed all of our clothes and set two alarms before laying down in bed. When all of the hustle of getting ready was done, I began to think of many things, but most of all I imagined what might happen the following day.

Liz and I kept asking each other, "Do you really think we're going to meet the Pope?" It didn't seem real. Be at the bronze doors was all the person had said. Could it be that they had called us with tickets to visit the crypt, not realizing that we had managed to get to see them the day before?

And as I lay there, thinking about meeting the Pope, I began to think about what I would do. This was my chance to ask for a miracle for Elie. Surely God would grant what the Holy Father asked. I lay back thinking how I might ask him, whether I would get close enough to ask him personally or whether I would have to call out from a pew.

Liz was thinking of me. I had once half-jokingly told Liz that if any of three conditions were met, I would become Catholic as she wished. First, if Elie were cured. Second, if Liz prayed so hard that she levitated. Or third, because I respected him so much, if the Pope personally asked me to become Catholic. On the last point, I told her a hand-written letter would be good enough since he was unlikely to want to call.

I was very facetious and probably too irreverent.

Now we might actually be meeting the Holy Father face-to-face, and Liz was trying to figure out how to ask him to ask me to become Catholic. I knew what she was thinking as we lay there, and I began to worry that we might only have a moment with him. I wanted to use that moment to talk about Elie and to ask for his prayers, not to talk about me. Elie was far more important.

I lay there in the darkness and the electricity between Liz and me was palpable. I was swept by these waves of chilling excitement as I imagined the following day. And fear also—I was filled with fear. The thought of standing before someone as holy as John Paul and asking for his prayers was thrilling and a little awesome.

"Liz," I said as we lay in the darkness. "Please don't ask the Pope to ask me to become a Catholic."

Silence.

"I want to talk to him about Elie. I want him to pray for Elie. Not about me."

Silence, and then Liz said, "Kent, you said if the Pope asked you to become Catholic, you would do it."

"I did, and I would," I said, "but you're not allowed to ask him to do it. We're going to see him because of Elie. Let's talk about Elie."

In the end, Liz agreed, though very reluctantly, and I was left in the darkness to think about how I would ask the Pope for a miracle and whether I would have the courage to follow through or the faith to believe a miracle could happen.

CHAPTER 20
John Paul II

In my imagination, John Paul is sitting beside the altar in St. Peters in a chair akin to the one our parish priest sits in during Mass. There are a hundred people in the pews. The chapel is ornate with a vaulted ceiling, and the altar lies beneath Bernini's canopy.

We are seated somewhere toward the back of the church. John Paul is a hundred feet away so that we can see him clearly, but we cannot really make out the expressions on his face.

He is listening to the second reading when suddenly I stand in my pew and begin to walk up the aisle. The lector stops reading and the church goes silent. As I approach John Paul, I kneel and climb the few steps on my knees. My head is bowed.

When I am directly in front of John Paul, I hold out a picture of Elie in both hands without looking up.

"Holy Father," I say. "This is my beautiful, only daughter and my first born and she is dying. She has a brain tumor. She cannot speak, eat, talk, walk, or take care of herself. She cannot smile at me or my wife. But we love her more than we could ever express."

"Holy Father," I say, bowing down before him, "I know God could heal her. I have asked for that many times. My wife and I have both asked God for a miracle, and Elie is still with us. But if you ask, God would not deny you. You are the holiest man on earth, and I know if you but ask God for a miracle, He will grant it to you."

"Please, Holy Father. Ask God to heal my beautiful child on our behalf."

As I re-imagine that hoped for scene even now, nearly eight years later, I am overcome with weeping.

※ ※

Liz and I woke and dressed in silence. We stepped out of the rear door of the apartment and let it swing closed behind us. The back of the palace opened onto a narrow labyrinth of alleys and streets, dimly lit by orange streetlamps. We turned left and walked briskly toward the corner where the alley opened into Piazza Venezia on the Via Florida. There, along the broad street, we picked up a waiting taxi. It was 5:20 am and, except for a few motos buzzing past, Rome was remarkably quiet.

The taxi dropped us at the front of St. Peter's Square. It was still dark and, here and there, people crossed the square in the shadows, their footsteps ringing out on the cobbles. Liz and I walked quietly toward the bronze doors at the far corner of the cathedral.

"Do you think we're right," I asked, almost in a whisper. "Are we really going to Mass with the Pope?"

"What else could it be," Liz said, just as quietly.

When we reached the end of the portico near the bronze doors, we paused and leaned against the nearest pillar. There was no one else around. The air was brisk. I shivered but not from the cold. Liz was saying the Rosary. I thought about what we wanted for Elie, how we wanted her to be made whole, not to lose her, for her to be a child who grows up—or even just a child who smiles at us.

"Do you think we're supposed to just wait here?" I asked.

"Shh," Liz said. "I'm praying."

I looked around and was surprised to see a priest standing now about 20 feet away against another pillar. He was reading a small book under the streetlamp. The sky was still dark and St. Peter's square was hushed.

As we stood there waiting, another small family arrived. The father wore a gray suit. The mother wore a dark dress. They had a girl with a ponytail that looked about twelve and a little boy who held on tight to his mother's hand. None of them spoke.

I nodded at them. When they drifted closer to us, I asked quietly, "Quanta hora hai?"

"I'm sorry," he said in a clipped Canadian accent, "I don't speak Italian."

I laughed. "Neither do I," I said. "I was hoping you would show me your watch so I could read the time."

It was 5:35 am.

More people began drifting toward us and aggregating in small knots. A few of the groups spoke in whispers amongst themselves. I noticed three or four more priests and a small family with a grandmother, mother and small boy. There was a priest with an older woman that looked like his mother. Two nuns stopped near our group.

I stepped away from the lamplight to look at the façade of St. Peter's, and I realized that the sky was just beginning to brighten, ever so slightly. The sense of trembling as we all waited hushed us to silence. It was like nothing I had ever experienced. I was still unsure we were actually going to attend Mass with the Pope, but the thought of it was unnerving. I reached instinctively into my wallet and pulled out a picture of Elie. In the photo, Liz is holding Elie cheek-to-cheek.

Liz looks wan and yellow. The photo is taken in her parents' driveway the day we drove Elie in for surgery.

"I'm going to show him Elie if we get a chance," I said.

"That's perfect," Liz said, "I wish she were here so we could introduce him."

I slipped the picture into my pocket and looked around. There were now nearly 20 people standing quietly and in small groups or families. A priest stood close to us. He stepped over and said quietly, "You sounded American. I just wanted to say hello."

"Hi Father," I said, shaking hands and introducing myself and Liz. "We are American. Are you too?"

"Charles Mangan," he said. "I'm from South Dakota, but for now I live here in Rome."

We spoke in a whisper for the next five minutes and learned about Father Mangan's duties and studies in Rome. He was an engaging and very warm man with a frank, open face and very polite manner.

"Sorry to interrupt, Father," I said after a moment or two, "but are you waiting here for the same reason we are waiting here."

"I assumed I was," he said with a quiet laugh. "Why are you waiting here?"

"We were called last night and asked to be at the bronze doors at 6 am," I said. "We think we may be going to Mass in St. Peter's with the Holy Father."

Father Mangan laughed again. "You are going to Mass with the Holy Father," he said. "But you are not going to St. Peter's. The Mass will be held in the Residence, in the Holy Father's private chapel."

I looked at Liz. She was smiling broadly. I realized I was gripping Elie's photo in my pocket so tightly that I was probably putting fingernails through the paper. We were going to meet the Holy Father. We were actually going to see him. I thought again about Elie, lying in a crib at home. It was my chance. I could ask for a miracle from the Holy Father, directly from the Holy Father. Be strong.

Father Mangan smiled again. He could sense my nervousness. "Don't worry," he said. "I can tell you a little about what will happen."

"Have you done this before?" I asked.

"A couple of times," he said. "At about 6 am, one of the members of the Papal household will invite us through the bronze doors into the Residence. They'll do a check of your passports, then we'll walk up some stairs and take an elevator to the top floor. We'll be invited into the Holy Father's chapel, where he will be in the middle of prayers."

"He is already in the middle of prayers?" Liz asked.

"They say he rises at 5 and prays until 7 or so, when morning Mass is finished," answered Father Mangan.

His voice trailed off and we stood together again in silence.

I am going to meet Pope John Paul II, I thought. Incredible. I will have the chance to ask for Elie's miracle of the most holy man on earth, from the direct representative of Jesus Christ. Incredible, I kept thinking. Incredible.

∽ ∾

The small clumps of people drifted toward the bottom of the steps before the bronze doors. At a little before six, one of the doors opened and a man stepped out. He was wearing a black suit with a short, clipped haircut.

"Buon Giorno," he said. "Viene, per piaceri." He motioned with his hand toward the door. "Come in," he added with a heavy Italian accent. We filed through the door in silence. Just inside the door were two of the Swiss guards in their bright uniforms. They sat on stools and nodded at us as we stepped through.

In front of us was a long, impossibly grand corridor. The roof stretched up in series of vaulted arches, supported by marble columns, as high as any cathedral ceiling I had ever seen. An enormous marble staircase wound up to the right some fifty feet along the hallway and wide enough for twenty people to climb abreast. The hallway itself lengthened out into the dim distance. Windows ran along the left wall, but the morning light was just beginning to show through them. Electric sconces shone dimly along the right wall.

We were ushered into a small ante chamber. The porter asked us for our passports, which we handed over. There was a wait of ten or fifteen minutes as they checked each passport against the invitations. We stood close to Father Mangan, and he told us about his diocese in South Dakota and some more about his work at the Vatican. I did not really register much of what he was saying. My mind kept leaping forward to the moment when we would meet John Paul. I tried to imagine it. Would I get to speak to him? Would he be separated from us? Should I approach him while he was praying? Would there be a time that was less disruptive? I heard little that Liz said. I stared over the heads of the other people. What would I do?

✧ ✧

When the passport checks were complete, the porter led us back into the hallway and up the grand marble staircase. At the top, we walked down a smaller corridor and into a gilded elevator. The porter pressed the button for the top floor.

We emerged into another hallway, this one with much lower ceilings and corridors that felt more like a personal residence in a grand mansion. The porter led us down a hall and into a large library. There were glass-encased bookshelves along the wall, and a very large, wooden desk with an opened atlas upon it. There was a beautiful antique globe in the corner. Two large windows opposite us looked out on St. Peter's Square.

"This is the Holy Father's personal library," said Father Mangan quietly to Liz and me. "They say he is the most widely traveled Pope in history and that he has been in front of more people than anyone else on earth. You can see his interests here," he indicated the globe and other maps with his hand, "in the globe and the atlas. I'm guessing he probably sits here to decide where he is going this year."

"Amazing," I said. Liz added something.

"Is this where he lives" I asked Father Mangan.

Father Mangan smiled at me. "It is," he said. "Pretty incredible being here, eh?"

"It's unbelievable," I answered. "I'm having trouble convincing myself that this isn't part of a dream."

We stood in the library for ten minutes. Nobody spoke above an occasional whisper. I suddenly began to feel that I looked far too shabby to be here. I wore a tweed jacket, but it had been through two weeks of suitcases, and the iron had not been able to erase its recent history. The Canadian father was in a gray suit. The priests all wore their black cleric's clothes, except for the Mexican priest who wore a light blue shirt with his white cleric's collar. I felt a little ashamed for not having brought better clothes.

A door opened in the corner of the room away from the windows. A priest with a full, round, Spanish-looking face stepped through. He propped the door open and put a finger to his lips as he walked along. He looked familiar, and I realized I had seen him serving the Pope before when Liz and I watched various papal addresses on TV. I wondered if he was the personal secretary to whom we had written.

"Take any stool," he said as he passed us. Then he said it again in Italian, then Spanish.

When he had passed all the way down line, he walked back up again with a finger to his lips. At the head of the line again, he motioned forward and the column of people began to move quietly down another hallway. Twenty feet down the hallway was a closed door on the right and an open one on the left. We turned into the open door and the sight that met us was one I shall never forget as long as I live.

The room was less than 30 feet long and perhaps 20 feet wide. The walls and floor were a luminescent marble. The ceiling was vaulted—twenty or so feet high. A steel, modern artistic Christ hung on a crucifix above the altar opposite us. And there, in the middle of the room, bent over a kneeler, obviously deep in prayer and facing away from us, was Pope John Paul II. He was three steps from me—ten feet away.

Just as everyone had done before me, I stopped dead in my tracks when I saw him. I felt frozen. The personal secretary stood at the side of the doorway. He took my arm gently and led me forward. There were five or six rows of very plain, three-legged stools. The first two rows had filled with the priests that accompanied us from downstairs. We filed into the third row and sat down. More people filled the rows behind us. Last, a group of eight or nine nuns who had not been waiting with us downstairs, filed in and took the row of stools against the rear wall. There were twenty-five of us in a small room with Pope John Paul.

And then we sat there. The Pope prayed earnestly. Most of the people in the room prayed, sitting on their stools. The stools were too close for anyone to get down on their knees. I could not pray. All I could think about was how I would ask the John Paul for a miracle. When should I ask him? I sat on my stool, frozen, watching the Pope at prayer.

He knelt and held his forehead in one hand. Every few minutes, he would wipe his hand across his face, look up, and then set his forehead back in his hand. He wore a cream-colored surplice that flowed out around his feet. The robes made him look quite broad, with wide shoulders. His hair was white and his scalp covered by a white skull cap. For long moments he was so still that it almost felt like we were all arranged behind a great, marble statue, then he would move and wipe his face again with his hand.

After thirty minutes or so, the aid to John Paul stepped up beside him and drew him carefully off his knees and onto the seat of the kneeler. One of the priests from the front row stood up and walked to a small podium in the corner. He read the first reading in Spanish and Mass began.

Father Mangan read one of the letters of St. Paul for the second reading. Then the Gospel in a central European language—I'm guessing Polish—from another priest in the front row. Mass proceeded, and I thought about when I might ask the Holy Father for a miracle for Elie. It seemed to me the best time would be when we approached him for Communion. It would be the least disruptive and I would already be near him. I waited with my hands gripped tightly at my side and my heart pounding.

During Communion, the Pope did not move forward. Instead his personal aid brought the Eucharist to him and then began to distribute it himself at the head of each row of people. I was on the end and crossed my arms across my chest as Liz had suggested to indicate that I could not participate, but he didn't understand me and tried to give the Eucharist to me anyway. I had to whisper to him that I was not Catholic, at which he looked very annoyed at me and moved on to Liz and the others behind her.

The incident was deflating. I thought, "What am I doing here?" and "Who am I to ask the Pope for a miracle." It was incredible the quickness with which doubt slipped into my mind and my resolve began to crumble. I hesitated. I wondered whether there would be a moment at all that would be less intrusive. I waited, and then Mass was over. The Pope was back on his kneeler, deep in prayer again and we were slowly filing out of the chapel, led by John Paul's aid. I looked back as I turned the corner. I had let my chance slip.

And then the group of us waited in the library again. Father Mangan was with his fellow priests at the head of what formed into something like a receiving line. The families who had attended the Mass were arranged at the back of the line near the exit to the library through which we had originally entered. Next to us were the German mother and grandmother with a little boy. He had fallen asleep across their laps during the Mass. Behind us was the Canadian family, standing very erect and in a tight group. Right next to us was the Mexican priest and his mother. We all waited. Liz said a few words, but I don't remember what she said.

We stood there for perhaps another thirty minutes. Then the personal aid clapped his hands softly at one end of the line. We all looked up, and the door to the chapel opened with John Paul shuffling slowly through. He stopped before each priest, said a few words to them, handed them each a set of Rosary beads in a small, brown purse. Slowly he worked his way down the line. Before each person, he stopped and spoke something to them, all in their own language. Just a few words. This was my chance.

When he reached the German grandmother just before us, he stooped down and tried to kiss the top of the little boy's head. The boy got frightened and pulled away to clutch at his mother's skirt. We all laughed, as did John Paul, then he reached out and touched the boy's head. He turned to Liz.

He was much smaller than I expected. With his natural stoop from age, his eyes were at the same height as Liz's. His left eye seemed opaque and blind, but his right eye was piercing. I waited, but when I looked down at Liz, she was softly crying and could not speak. Her hands moved as if to try and loosen her voice, but she could say nothing. I stepped forward.

"Holy Father," I said, pulling the picture of Elie from my pocket and holding it out to her. "This is my daughter."

He looked at the picture, then briefly up at me, and then he looked at Liz again. He stared at her, then spoke.

"What's the matter with her?" he asked in a heavy European accent.

"She has a brain tumor," I said, a little awed by our conversation. I felt some of Liz's constriction. It was hard to talk.

"What?" he said and turned to his personal aid.

"A brain tumor," I said at the same time as the personal aid said, "Tumore" in Italian.

"Oh," said John Paul.

He reached out and stroked Liz's face gently, then he handed both of us Rosary beads. "You two should pray together," he said.

And then my moment was gone forever. I knew somehow that I had failed. John Paul was moving down the line fairly quickly now. At the end of the line, he said thank you to us for coming to Mass with him, then exited back toward the chapel. Everyone clapped and within moments we were heading back out the way we had come.

All I could think about was that I had failed. I began to rationalize it almost immediately. The time had never really been right. I thought I would get a moment more, but he spoke to Liz the whole time. I was foolish to think I could ask him for a miracle at all. On and on, but as I look back, I realize my doubt collapsed my will. I hesitated because I doubted. Liz failed to speak because she believed. I failed because I did not.

> *Just as he was speaking, the rooster crowed. The Lord turned and looked straight at Peter. Then Peter remembered the word the Lord had spoken to him: "Before the rooster crows today, you will disown me three times." And he went outside and wept bitterly.*

What was it like for Peter to face Jesus' baleful glance, knowing that he had failed because of his inner doubts?

I think I know.

I also think I know what Peter felt when he recalled Jesus' other words. "When you have turned back, strengthen your brothers."

God gave Peter a lifetime to make up for his weakness and failure. God grant us all such a reprieve.

CHAPTER 21
Requiem

Elizabeth Nyanga Gilges died on March 11, 2004 on my lap, cradled between Liz and me.

She died quietly, peacefully. As she breathed her last few breaths, Liz said a Hail Mary and cried out, "Jesus come!" I whispered in her small ear, "Elie. Go, beautiful. Go to God. Go." She took a half breath, shuddered once almost imperceptibly as if her body held very lightly now to her soul, took another half breath, and then she breathed no more.

We bathed her, combed out her hair, dressed her in a blue Easter dress that Liz's brother had bought for her, and placed her in the coffin which we as a family had made.

It was built of ash, painted white with a black inlaid cross on the cover. The inside was lined with white satin. The children each placed two hand prints in bright colors on the side of the coffin and wrote underneath in black marker, "I love you, Elie," and their name.

In the morning, Liz's mother and her sister brought a tiara made of yellow and blue flowers and we placed it on her forehead before the wake. Never have I seen anything more beautiful than her face in the dim twilight of her room.

Requiem in Pace. Is Elie resting in peace? I guess I hope not. I hope that for the first time, a little girl who was never able to walk finally has the use of her legs and is running through fields filled with the yellow and blue flowers that adorned her pale brow as she lay in her coffin.

The night Elie died, we tried to explain to our children again what death meant. They all listened solemnly. When we were done with our explanation, there were a few moments of quiet, then four year-old Hannah asked us: "Mom, can Elie do a cartwheel now?"

There is a deep cleft of sorrow caused by her absence. While still full, our days seem at times bereft of something fine and beautiful that once filled them to overflow, our home seems diminished. As difficult as it was when I was tired to go downstairs and hold Elie in the evening, make small conversation with her nurses, make sure she was warm and comfortable, I realize now the beautiful gift of knowing without any doubt that I could make one person's life better each day.

Often I would walk down to her room at 9:30 or 10 o'clock, and Elie would be lying on her back with her eyes wide open, looking up at the ceiling. The nurse would be mixing medicines. The feeding pump would be running slowly and the TV would be on. I would sneak up on the side of her bed, kiss her on the cheek and nestle my nose into her neck to kiss her again, and I would say, "Elie, do you want me to pick you up and we'll watch a ballgame together?" And then I would wait, because it always took a little bit for her, as if she were switching the brain pathways manually. And then, after a moment or two, she would give a big sigh.

There is a deep cleft of sorrow in her absence. Yes, but somewhere far beneath the sorrow there is an abiding pool of peace. Subterranean perhaps, at times it is hard to find, but when I climb deepest into my sorrow, when it feels very dark indeed, then, at the fundament of the soul, I find this pool.

I hope that as the pool rises in the coming time, it may fill the space left by Elie's absence with some sort of joy that transcends her loss.

CHAPTER 22
Miracles

There were so many times we asked God for a miracle. I think back to my evening in Michigan, standing before the plate glass window, when I asked for a sign. I think about our trip to Lourdes, our stubborn insistence that God "heal" our little girl, as if she weren't whole as she was. Liz always added, "If it is your will..." but we hoped that healing Elie was His will.

But then I think about the first moments in Ann Arbor as we knelt over her bed, knowing that we would lose her to a brain tumor, knowing that the tumor had already caused a mini-stroke and that it would end her life soon.

And what I asked for, what we both asked for at that moment, wasn't healing but time. In the urgency of those first moments when we were desperate, we asked for more time with Elie. I remember Liz crying and saying that she couldn't imagine going home to an empty house with no children. She begged God not to take Elie until we had another child. I asked for just a couple of years. Please God, let us have her for just a couple of years.

As a father now with six children, I am able to recognize the different ways children cry. I can distinguish one cry from another—when they are crying for what they want and when they cry for what they need—and I react differently to those two cries. It is not right for me to respond to everything my child wants, for that could spoil their character. But I try always to respond to what my child needs, for that is compelled by my love for them.

I imagine God, as Father, is loving and compassionate in the same way.

Perhaps we received the miracle which we needed if not the miracle which we wanted. Time. We asked for Elie to be healed. That was what we wanted, but God knew that what we really needed was time with her. He gave us what we needed, ten glorious and lovely years. The doctors in Ann Arbor suggested she would live six months. The doctors in New York, even after her surgery, told us she might live 18 months, a few years at the outside. Elie lived ten full years with us and had four brothers and a sister before she died.

If time with Elie was her first miracle, it was not her last. I hope that Elie can at last run in the fields of Heaven. If she can, then I am sure, as God's handmaiden, she is deeply engaged in His work and engaged with the very people who cared for her while she was with us. The intimations of her enduring presence are already there.

※ ※

Father Mike concelebrated Elie's funeral Mass. The funeral was on Saturday, and he had to leave immediately that afternoon to celebrate Mass in his parish on Sunday. After he returned home to Michigan, he called to relate the following story.

His flight home to Escanaba took him through the Detroit airport, where the second leg of his flight was cancelled. At the gate for his flight to Marquette, he met by chance a small group of acquaintances who also were flying north. They decided to go to an airport cafe and have a sandwich together while they waited for the next flight.

In the café, Father Mike recognized one of the waitresses serving other tables. He was sure he had seen her on a trip he had made the year before. The waitress, who was Indian or Pakistani, was so strikingly beautiful that she stood out in his memory, the way a painting or a photograph sometimes imprints an image in your mind. Only once before had he been to this café, yet he remembered this particular waitress.

After his acquaintances returned to the gate, Father Mike lingered at the table. He told us later he felt like he was supposed to talk to the woman.

I should say that Father Mike is as chaste and proper a man and priest as I have ever met, and so he must have felt a little conflicted in his compelling urge to talk to this beautiful woman when he thought about the impression he would give her or others in the café who watched him, dressed in cleric's clothes, approach her. I imagine that is why he lingered, uncertain how to proceed.

Nevertheless, when Father Mike finished his coffee, he stood up and walked to the serving area where the short-order cook was lining up the breakfasts for the waitress to bring out. She was bustling around, putting orders in, totaling a table's check, getting coffee mugs for customers who had just sat down.

"Excuse me," said Father Mike, "but I just wanted to introduce myself. I'm Father Mike Steber and, it may sound funny, but I was in this restaurant a year ago and I recognized you."

She said nothing and he continued. "It probably sounds odd, and please don't take this in the wrong way, but you are really very beautiful, and I just recognized you from so long ago and felt like I was supposed to introduce myself..."

"I'm sorry, Father," she said, "I don't remember you. So many people come through here. A year is a long time…"

"Oh, that's okay. There's no way you would remember me. I didn't expect that. May I ask your name?"

She paused and brushed her hair back from her face with the back of her hand. "Ellie," she said.

Father Mike just stared at her for a moment, surprised by her name. After a long pause, he asked, "Is there something you would like me to pray for?"

She hesitated again and looked at him, as if testing whether she could really trust him. Finally she said, "Yes. Could you please pray for my mother. She just lost a son."

Father Mike nodded, blessed her, and left.

There are no coincidences. Has Elie already begun her work?

❧ ☙

One of Liz's closest friends was diagnosed with a rare and aggressive form of mouth cancer this year. She is tall, young, and beautiful with a lovely, optimistic view of life, and she has three girls about the same age as our own children, including twins, which is how we met.

After a surgery, which removed much of her palette, and radiation that essentially burned her mouth and throat in the hopes of killing remaining cancer cells, Mary was in a lot of pain. She could not swallow, her mouth was always dry because her saliva glands were destroyed, the prosthesis which was constructed to replace her palette caused its own pain. Mary was on tube feeding and had lost nearly 20 percent of her weight because she could not handle any food. She was tired and spent much of every day lying in bed with no energy to move.

Before the surgery, Mary had such a zest for life. Afterwards, there were times when she showed little interest in living. Her energy was gone. Her waking hours were dominated by lethargy and disinterest. She found little pleasure in anything.

Liz was one of the people that took Mary to her radiation appointments at the hospital and, though Mary has a spirit that is irrepressible, each evening Liz would come home sad because one of her very best friends was enduring so much. I often heard Liz praying for Mary when she sat with Elie on her lap in the evenings, and Elie would lie on Liz's lap with her eyes wide open, smacking her lips together as she often did.

The radiation treatments ended in February, but the pain in Mary's mouth increased to the point that Mary had real difficulty taking out the prosthesis even to clean it as she was supposed to do twice a day. We were concerned that Mary had become so thin and that, if she were to get sick with something as little as a cold or the flu, it could be fatal. Liz drove to Mary's house a couple of times to help her with the tube feedings since it was second nature to us, but could easily be scary for someone not used to it.

And then Elie became ill, and the illness was diagnosed as a septic infection of her bowels, and we realized with a jolt that Elie would only be with us for a few days. Our time and care was taken with Elie's final hours and making her comfortable until her death, which happened on a Thursday.

After the Saturday funeral and most of our family had left to return home, Mary called Liz. They talked for a long time about a range of things. After they hung up, Liz found me in the living room, reading a book. She was smiling and her eyes were filled with tears.

"You're not going to believe this," she said.

I put down my book as Liz spoke. "Mary began eating food yesterday evening... by mouth. She ate a full meal. The pain in her mouth is completely gone." Liz beamed radiantly at me.

"Completely gone?" I asked.

"Completely."

"That's great," I said.

Liz stared at me. "It's Elie," Liz said. "Mary and I decided it was Elie's first miracle. She's taking care of us now."

∽ ∾

My grandfathers both died when I was 12 years old. Both were wonderful men, but the one to whom I was closest was my mother's father. He was the one who took me fishing for the first time. We camped in an Indian teepee and went owling in the deep woods at night. He taught me about hunting and how to shoot skeet and trap. He walked me through the deep ravine in his back yard, showed me the shed skins of black rat snakes, pulled the roots of sassafras for me to chew on, rode me around on his tractor, let me stand in the garden and bother him while he picked green beans for dinner. He instilled in me the deep love of the outdoors that probably in large measure shaped my future.

I used to visit him for a few weeks each summer. He took me to my first Cleveland Indians baseball game and let me tag along with him on his trips to the hardware store, where he always sweet talked the cashiers who were at least 40 years younger than him.

When he died, I was really heartbroken for a while. In my sadness, I brought my dog, a beagle named Hunter, into my bedroom to lie in bed with me. The dog, a very independent sort, usually could only stand about three minutes next to me before finding a corner of the room to curl up and go to sleep himself. And I would cry and think about how much Grandpa had meant to me.

A month or so after my grandfather died, he visited me in a dream one night. In the dream, I was lying in bed. My grandmother, who was still alive, was sitting on another bed in the room, and Grandpa sat down beside me and talked to me for what seemed a long time. He held my hand and told me that everything was fine and there was no reason for me to be sad. He spoke to me until I had run out of questions, and then I awoke.

I sat up in bed in the middle of my dark room, and I remember that the memory of his exact words and our conversation faded as my eyes opened. Yet the memory of his visit and the comfort that I felt afterward have never left me. It is still vivid today, decades later.

I recount this because it left with me the indelible impression that spirits are real and that there can be interaction between the living and the dead. And I recount it for two other reasons.

First, because I have clung to the hope that Elie would visit me—even just once—in a dream to let me know she was well. I cling to that hope, though she has not come to me.

Second, because she has visited Liz.

The day after Elie died, we were busy with so many things. Preparations for her funeral, visitation by friends and family at our home where Elie was laid in her room in the casket. We were both heavily weighed down with our own sense of loss and yet Liz clearly carried a feeling of joy.

I asked Liz at one point, between visitation periods at the wake, why she seemed so happy. She turned to me with a smile and said, "You're going to think this is crazy." She paused, then continued, "but Elie has been talking to me this whole time. Everybody is moving around, and I'm greeting people, but I can hear a high-pitched, excited voice all around me. She keeps saying, 'Hi, Mommy. Hello Mommy." Liz's eyes filled with tears and she turned away. "It sounds crazy," she said, "but I feel like she is hugging me. I feel like she is really there."

"It doesn't sound crazy," I said. I told her about my grandfather, a story I had never told anyone. When I was done, I said, "I wish Elie would visit me. Just one more time."

Since that day, Liz has heard Elie's voice four more times. The second time was at the burial. The third, fourth, and fifth times were at church during Holy Week—Wednesday during Adoration in the evening, Thursday at the Mass for the Last Supper, and Good Friday. The last three times, Elie spoke to her briefly, saying the same thing, "Hi Mommy. Hello Mommy," for a few minutes. Liz answered quietly, under her breath, and sometimes only in prayer, "Hello Elie."

Afterwards, Liz was very peaceful.

※ ※

Liz's best friend is named Catherine. They have been friends since second grade. Through most of our marriage, I have wondered—and hesitated to ask Liz—if Catherine is a closer friend than me. I have my suspicions, which is why I have never asked.

Catherine married a wonderful man named Brad, and they had a first child named William after nine months of marriage—a honeymoon baby.

Their second baby did not come. Even after many trying months, and then years, of fertility work, drugs, procedures, it looked as if they were unable to conceive another child. The first pregnancy had caused Catherine's body to change so that they apparently could not conceive.

They began to explore adoption. Another year passed as they waited for a child. Two babies were promised them, but the birth mothers decided to keep the babies at the last moment. It was heart wrenching to watch the process. I have trouble imagining what it was like for them living it. Finally, they adopted a very healthy and rambunctious boy whom they named John. Their first son was already seven. Catherine, who just like Liz had always wanted a large family, resigned herself to two children. She told Liz just before Elie died that she could not go through the adoption process again. It was too difficult.

The weekend Elie died, Brad and Catherine came for the wake and funeral. I was sitting aside because I really did not want to talk to people, but Liz was deep in conversation with Catherine. Later, she told me that they had talked about Catherine having more children.

"Catherine," Liz said, "pray to Elie. Ask her to intercede with God on your behalf and ask for twins. She's in heaven. She can intervene for you now. It's possible. Pray to Elie."

A month later Catherine called us. She was pregnant. With twins.

◈ ◈

Yann Martel wrote a wonderful book called "The Life of Pi" in which he recounted, from a small boy's perspective, spending 270 days marooned in a lifeboat with a Bengal tiger. He begins by saying, "I will tell you a story that will make you believe in God," and, in the end, he does so.

The way he makes good on his promise is that he offers a wonderful story that is almost impossible to believe and yet it is plausible enough that you *want* to believe it. Then, at the end, he offers a grim version of the same story that is much easier to believe and in which, the character of the tiger, the many events in the boat, and other characters in the story are actually allegory for real human acts of horrible savagery and brutality, changed by a boy to protect himself psychologically.

Then the storyteller asks, "Which do you choose to believe? In the one version life is quite beautiful and full of mystery. Why would you choose to believe the other if it just makes life ugly."

It is a beautiful parable of faith. We believe not because we can prove it logically, not because it makes us better people—although it certainly does that—and not, in the end, because we have no choice. (I am reminded of Isaac Bashevis Singer's wonderful paradox: We must believe in free-will; we have no choice). We believe because it fills our lives with depth, and mystery and beauty.

I believe Elie has talked to Liz because Liz told me it happened and because it fills my heart with a sense of wonder and beauty.

I believe Elie is now engaged in the work of ministering to the broad family she built around her during her time with us, the many people she touched and who cared or prayed for her: building our faith, easing our sorrows, protecting the people we love.

I believe in God because it makes my life more interesting, less rational, and, finally, more worthwhile. I believe in God because my heart—not my head—tells me it is true.

CHAPTER 23
Purposes

I find myself often wondering how to answer the question from my oldest son, Alexander. He asked with the poignant innocence borne of not really understanding the permanence behind the question: "Dad, why did Elie have to die?"

The question may have no good answer, but it troubles me mainly because if there is an answer, it is hidden in the antipode: "Why did Elie live?"

What was the purpose of her life?

People of great faith have frequently offered to Liz and me that there must be a purpose to Elie's sacrifice, that—perhaps—she is leading others closer to God through this suffering. I have myself looked for solace in this thought at times.

There is a sort of numb comfort offered in the bromide that everything has a purpose and that Elie's suffering in some way contributes to a greater whole, yet when I follow that logic deeper, I find it very troubling. As far as we know, Elie could never make choices herself, so at some level it indicates that Elie's sacrifice was a choice made by God and that God makes sacrifices of individuals on behalf of the greater good. I do not believe that is possible.

With two monumental exceptions, God does not condone, create, or allow suffering by an individual in order to advance a good in another sphere. The sacrifice of one for the good of the many is a human construct. It is a human choice. God does not choose "between the lesser of two evils" because that would imply that God could choose an evil. God always chooses good, and His care is ever for the dignity, worth, and aid of the individual. I cannot believe that God, in His goodness, would pick Elie out of a row of souls and deign that she shall suffer for ten years no matter what "good" it might create on the backside.

One of the most striking aspects of the Gospels is the ever-present focus on the individual. The acts of Jesus' mercy demonstrate above all else the care that God takes for the individual. When He is surrounded by masses of people, all of whom look to him for something, He parts the crowd and ministers to the one—Bartimaeus, the Roman centurian's servant, Jairus' daughter, Lazarus, the blind beggar. Again, with two exceptions, God never sacrifices the one for the good of the many.

The first exception that God allows, the sacrifice of Jesus, is monumental because in choosing to sacrifice an individual on behalf of the many, God chooses Himself as the sacrifice. He cannot choose an evil—the evil of sacrificing an individual for mankind's benefit—so he becomes a man. He chooses to sacrifice Himself.

The second sacrifice I only realized the night Liz sat with Elie dying on her lap. God asks Mary to make the sacrifice of her son. Jesus is not only God's son. God chose a mother to carry the child, and the sacrifice is not just of God for mankind, but indirectly of the mother who must watch the child die. God must have felt great pity and sorrow for what He asked of Mary.

What is the purpose of Elie's suffering?

I don't think there is a purpose or a plan to her suffering. She suffered because she was born, because she lived. We all suffer. It is the payment we make for the great gift of life.

What is the purpose of Elie's life?

That is the great mystery. That is the mystery that I spend much of my spiritual thought trying to understand. The question is one we all end up asking of ourselves. What is the purpose of my life? God did not sacrifice Elie in order that He might bring me, or you, or anyone closer to Him. She lived, suffered, died, and was buried. As I will. As you will.

We each walk our own path as individuals. Those paths cross numerous others. We are shaped by the crossings, but we choose our own path, we live our own lives, we endure our own sufferings. God cares for those individual paths. The purpose of each individual life, as best I can surmise, is to regain paradise, each as individuals. If sacrifice is involved—to help others on the same journey—it is an individual's choice. It is pleasing to God, but it is not His to choose for us.

C.S. Lewis wrote:

> *Isn't God supposed to be good? Isn't he supposed to love us? And does God want us to suffer? What if the answer to that question is yes? See, I'm not sure that God wants us to be particularly happy. I think he wants us to love and to be loved. He wants us to grow up. I suggest to you that it is because God loves us that he gives us the gift of suffering. Or to put it another way, pain is God's megaphone to rouse a deaf world. You see, we are like blocks of stone out of which The Sculptor carves the forms of man. The blows of His chisel which hurt us so much are what makes us perfect.*

I cannot help but repeat what Pearl Buck wrote of her own disabled daughter because it so perfectly captures the essence of this idea: "There must be acceptance and the knowledge that sorrow fully accepted brings its own gifts. For there is an alchemy in sorrow. It can be transmuted into wisdom, which, if it does not bring joy, can yet bring happiness."

Elie is the greatest gift we as a family could have received. She made—and still makes—our lives far richer, more contemplative, and full of joy than they ever would have been without her. She was a beloved and essential part of our family and would have been as long as she was with us. Elie has given us an awareness of suffering's noble beauty.

Suffering is the payment for life? Sacrifice is the choice of the individual, not the plan by God? I don't know. I just don't know. It is a paradox.

Perhaps that is my answer to my child's question—a paradox: "Alex, life is so good that I'm dying to find out what it all means."

Order Form

To order please complete and mail to:
CIDER PRESS PUBLISHING,
P.O. BOX 262,
CANANDAIGUA, NY 14424

Name _____
Address _____
City _____
State _____ Zip _____

Email: _____

# of Books _____ x $18.95 = _____

Shipping & Handling $4.90

Add $2 for each additional Book   _____

Subtotal   _____

NYS Residents Add Tax 7.125%   _____

Total Enclosed
(check or money order)   _____

A GRACE GIVEN

Kent Gilges

279 pages
Size 5.25 x 8
ISBN 13: 978-0-615-17626-0

Cider Press Publishing
Trade Paperback
$18.95
Publication date: 3/2008

A Grace Given
Kent Gilges

There is a blessing sent from God in every burden of sorrow. There is hope in that, hope even to a dying child.

---

www.ciderpresspublications.com
Cider Press Publishing
P.O. Box 262, Canandaigua, NY 14424